MARIE BRUCE

FIRST STEPS TO

Solitary
Witchcraft

Dedication

This book is dedicated to my best friends and sisters in witchcraft, Dawn Marie and Keeley Ann. I am truly grateful for your friendship and all your support.

A special thank you goes to Dawny (*aka* Aurora) for writing the poem 'The Triple Goddess' especially for inclusion in this book. Thanks a mil', honey. You're a gem!

With lots of love to you both
from Maz

MARIE BRUCE

FIRST STEPS TO
Solitary Witchcraft

Its practice and life benefits

quantum
LONDON • NEW YORK • TORONTO • SYDNEY

quantum

An imprint of W. Foulsham & Co. Ltd
The Publishing House, Bennetts Close, Cippenham, Slough,
Berkshire, SL1 5AP, England

ISBN 0-572-03068-1

Cover artwork by Jurgen Ziewe

A CIP record for this book is available from the British Library

Printed in Great Britain by St Edmundsbury Press Ltd, Bury St Edmunds, Suffolk

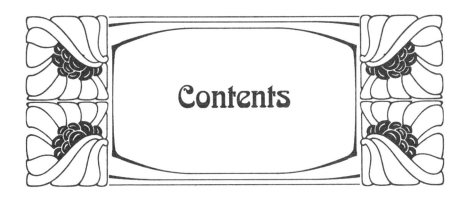

Contents

Witch

Find me in the story books,
The fairy-tales, the history books;
See me everywhere you look;
    Hear the folk cry, 'Witch!'
Picture me flying through the night,
Broomstick flight through starry night,
Gleaming with enchanted light;
    Gasp and then cry, 'Witch!'
See the wood begin to burn;
Nowhere to run, nowhere to turn;
Thumbscrews and the rack they turn
    Before they burn the witch.
Goddess worship underground;
Don't make a noise, don't make a sound;
Must not tell or they'll know they've found
    A woman who's a witch.
End the deaths and end the rage
With the dawn of a New Age;
Cleanse the past with burning sage
Bought from a store called WITCH.
In open rites the pagans sing,
Casting a sacred circle ring.
'They say Wicca is the next big thing!'
    Hail a new kind of witch.
But they don't know what pagans know,
What I know and what you now know,
    That witchcraft only went below
And that there's always been the witch!

Morgana

A Woman's Wisdom

omen have always been powerful. Through the ages women have been midwives, healers, warriors, shamans, priestesses, queens and – of course – witches. In the modern world, women have taken on the roles of doctor, solicitor, judge, company director, film star, musician, soldier, police officer, fire fighter, provider, breadwinner and many more.

Today's women enjoy more freedom of choice than our gender has ever known before. Why then do so many women still feel powerless? Why are we fearful that we won't be able to make ends meet, be a good parent or overcome a particular challenge in life?

And why do so many of us struggle to embrace the term 'self-acceptance' and yet will willingly shoulder the burden of 'failure'? Perhaps it is because modern women have lost touch with the natural wisdom our ancestors had in abundance – the wisdom of feminine power, divine inner beauty and natural magic. In short, the power of witchcraft!

If you long to throw out the fashion magazines and feel beautiful and sexy no matter what ... if you want your man to look at you and no other and be completely captivated by your feminine allure ... if you want to feel the power of magic tingling through your fingertips so you can rise to whatever challenge life hurls at you ... then this is definitely the book for you! Take back your power as a woman, realise your own unique potential and live the life of a goddess! With the help of this book you need never feel powerless again. Unlock the secrets of solitary witchcraft and release your inner magic. Welcome to the Craft!

Blessed be!

Morgana

Witchcraft
Past and Present

Witchcraft is an enjoyable and empowering practice that gets massive results. It is a positive path to spirituality and connection with deity, and it can be used to improve your life beyond recognition. Witchcraft teaches that we all have the right to everything the universe has to offer: love, prosperity, balance, friendship, happiness, security, peace of mind and so on.

Humankind are creatures of divinity in that we all hold a spark of divine power within us. Unfortunately, many people never fully realise the potential they hold within themselves, and as a result may often feel helpless and hopeless. Witchcraft, however, teaches us how to tap into this power and use it positively, for the greater good of all and with harm to none.

First Steps to Solitary Witchcraft was written for all those women who are looking for a life-enhancing way to develop their own personal power and achieve their goals, while at the same time increasing their sense of spirituality and feminine wisdom. We will explore ways of developing and maintaining independence, defining personal boundaries and attaining personal goals. We will also look at what it means to be a woman in today's world, exploring various female roles along the way. And we will discover what being a witch really means.

You will no doubt have your own perception of what a witch is. You will have come across her in your childhood story books. Maybe she was flying through the air on a broomstick, or perhaps she was holding out a shiny red apple, laced with poison, to tempt you into her pretty little cottage made from gingerbread and icing sugar. You will have seen the witch on the silver screen, frantically chasing Dorothy for her beautiful ruby slippers, or joining hands in a circle of friends to lift a love curse. On the small screen, witches appear as three gorgeous women in an attic, vanquishing evil demons and warlocks, and as the enthusiastic blonde teenager whispering secrets into the ears of a talking cat.

Witches and witchcraft have always captured the imagination and have been the inspiration behind great poems, plays and paintings. But is there a truth hidden within the fairy-tales, the blockbuster movies and the cult TV shows? The answer to this question is undoubtedly – yes! In this book we will be exploring both the myth and the magic of witchcraft and the spirituality of the Old Ways.

The spirituality of the Craft

Witchcraft is a way of life. It is a spiritual belief system (or religion) that respects the Earth and the natural world around us, that honours all women and that reveres the divine feminine, known to witches as the Great Mother Goddess. We will be looking in depth at the Goddess in the next chapter, but for now suffice it to say that goddess-based religions such as witchcraft and paganism place women in a position of undisputed power and authority.

As witches, we live our religion every day, casting spells and making magic to help both ourselves and others. We practise rituals in reverence and give thanks for all the good things we have. We use our magic and our power to overcome life's little problems, such as paying bills, finding love, communicating with people and so on. We also work global magic, casting spells to bring world peace, end terrorism, purify our rivers and oceans, protect endangered species and send out healing love after a natural disaster. On a personal level we work magic to protect ourselves and our loved ones, our pets, homes and property; to help heal a sick relative; to attune with our own higher self; and to become proactive within our own lives.

Witches don't sit around waiting for our dreams to be handed to us, for life just to happen to us. Witches make things happen by taking control of our own lives, accepting personal responsibility and creating our own destiny as much as we can. In all of these things magic is a key component.

Witchcraft works and witches do exist. I am a practising solitary witch and I know my Craft is real. I cast spells regularly, I observe the sabbats of the Wheel of the Year, and I perform rituals on the 13 esbats (or full moons).

I am a more balanced and fulfilled person because I am a witch, and I have said on more than one occasion that witchcraft is one of the best things that has ever happened to me. Hopefully, by the end of this book it will be one of the best things that has ever happened to you too.

Now, I am not saying that my life is absolutely perfect and that I have nothing to work for, nothing to strive for. Witchcraft is not a quick fix. What I am saying is that witchcraft is the support system and the tool that I use to deal with the imperfections in my life. What witches don't like, we change. If we cannot change something, then we learn to accept it. We change ourselves and our attitude so that we can adapt to life's circumstances.

Being a witch is not easy. In fact, it's a full-time occupation. But the rewards are immense and well worth all the effort that learning the Craft demands. Being a witch means taking responsibility for each of your thoughts, words and actions. Witches tend not to blame their problems on outside circumstances such as an unhappy childhood. Instead, they see negative situations as a challenge they can overcome and a chance to grow stronger as an individual.

We witches have a saying that goes 'once a witch, always a witch'. This refers to our belief in reincarnation. So if you feel drawn to witchcraft at this point in your life, there is a strong chance that you have been on this path in a previous life or that witchcraft is somehow in your blood.

Because witchcraft is a very time-consuming activity, and because great power comes only with much practice and application, only a true witch will have the dedication it takes to learn our Craft. The rest will fall by the wayside. Witchcraft is not the route to a quick-fix power trip. The Goddess knows and recognises her own, and has a way of winnowing out any who are seeking magical powers for the wrong reasons.

So if you plan to use magic for negative means, put this book down. You are on the wrong path. But if you feel the rhythms of nature beating in your heart, gaze in wonder at the beauty of the full moon and wish to empower yourself as a woman, working for the greater good of all, then read on ... for you are already a witch!

Paganism

Witchcraft is a branch of paganism. It is an Earth-based, goddess-centred religion which honours and respects matriarchy, rather than the patriarchal rule that Christianity and most other orthodox religions teach. Simply put, pagans believe in a female form of divinity – to us, God is a woman!

Of course, pagans understand that in order for life to be constantly recreated, both male and female energies must be present, and they therefore honour both the feminine and the masculine – the Goddess and the God. This is recognised as the polarity in all things. However, most pagans focus more on the Goddess as the primary creator and ultimate source of life.

All witches are pagans, but not all pagans are witches. Some are druids (members of witchcraft's sister tradition). Others are neo-pagan or eco-pagan and focus their attention on ecological and green issues rather than magic and ritual. Still others prefer to call themselves simply 'pagan' and do not adhere to any particular magical tradition beyond the general nature-based pagan principles. There are many excellent books on the subject of paganism in all its forms, so if this area interests you, visit your library or local book store and see what you can find. *Listening People, Speaking Earth* by Graham Harvey is a good overview.

A brief history of witchcraft

Everyone knows that witches were persecuted, tortured, hanged and burnt at the stake. And every modern witch is thankful that such dangerous times are well and truly past, for now she can sleep easy in her bed and practise her Craft without fear of condemnation.

I feel it is important for any new witch to know something about the path the Craft has taken through history, for – as with any culture or religion – to appreciate it fully in the here and now, you must first understand and acknowledge its history and heritage. As you will see, the history of witchcraft is both a fascinating and a disturbing one.

Around 25,000 years ago, humankind worshipped the God of the Hunt and the Goddess of Fertility. These two deities are the forerunners of the witches' God and Goddess. Men were responsible for hunting for food that was vital to the survival of the tribe, and they invoked the God of the Hunt to help them in this task. We know from prehistoric cave paintings that they did this by enacting the stalking of the prey, wearing a head-dress of antlers or horns to take on the appearance of the Horned God himself. This ritual is now thought to be the oldest form of sympathetic magic (a magic that works on the basis that like attracts like) ever performed.

Offerings were made to the Goddess of Fertility to ensure that there would continue to be animals to hunt (and, in later prehistory, crops in the field). She was seen as the source of all life and was often represented as pregnant and large-breasted. Goddess images were often decorated with fertility symbols such as eggs, fish and moon symbols (connecting them to the lunar-linked cycle of menstruation and ovulation).

These two nature deities were worshipped, in various forms, all over the world for millennia – until the advent of the new patriarchal religions, such as Judaism and Christianity. For Christians, the Old Religion – the worship of the nature deities, or witchcraft and paganism, as it came to be known in Europe – became a rival faith.

In order to convert the pagan masses to the new Christian religion, its priests built their churches on old pagan sites and absorbed much of the iconography of the Old Religion into their own faith. The pagan calendar of sacred sabbats was embossed with new Christian holidays. In this way Yule became Christmas, Imbolc became Candlemas, Beltane was pushed forward slightly and became May Day, and the witches' harvest festival of Samhain became All Hallow's Eve (or Halloween). This last was portrayed as a night of demons, devils and evil. Thus the first seed of fear of witches and magic was cleverly planted.

As Christianity expanded and grew in strength and power, the Horned God of the old religion became known as the devil of the new faith. He was given a new name, Satan, and those pagans and witches who continued to invoke him became known as 'devil worshippers' – people to be feared and exposed to punishment. If such people refused to be converted to the new faith and continued to cling to the Old Ways, as many of them did, they were said to be possessed by the devil and were hunted down and exterminated.

During the Middle Ages, fear of magic and witches grew increasingly in Europe. In 1486 this widespread terror was given impetus when two German monks, Heinrich Kramer and Jakob Sprenger, provided an instruction manual specifically for the prosecution of witches. The book was called the *Malleus Maleficarum* or *The Hammer of Witches*. This anti-witch volume was soon available throughout Europe, and it left in its wake a trail of blood, persecution and torture. The *Malleus Maleficarum* was the bestseller of the medieval period, and it played a significant part in the death of an estimated nine million people. The witch hunt had begun.

The Burning Times

The Burning Times is the name given to the period in history when witches, and especially female witches, were ruthlessly persecuted and killed. Most modern-day witches cannot mention the Burning Times without a shiver of fear running down their spine. It is the darkest hour of the Craft, and the darkest period in Western history for womankind.

Within the pages of the *Malleus Maleficarum* were instructions on how to detect, try, torture and execute an accused witch. The book stated that witches were responsible for failure of crops, infertility in women, impotence in men, sickness in livestock, cot deaths, still births, the sacrifice of babies and the promiscuity of husbands, as well as foul weather conditions and natural disasters. The book also promulgated the biggest misconception of all: that witches are evil devil worshippers who use magic to harm and control others. In fact, nothing could be further from the truth, but this ill-founded belief is one that modern witches are still fighting against today, more than 500 years after the *Malleus Maleficarum* was published.

During the sixteenth and seventeenth centuries, the witch hunt continued at full cry in Britain, with King James I passing the Witchcraft Act in 1604, making all practice of the Craft illegal. In this climate, the occupation of witch finder could often prove to be prosperous employment. The most notorious of the witch finders was a man called Mathew Hopkins, who became known as the Witch Finder General because of his vigilance in his task. He was the terror of women in East Anglia, and often proved to be their death. It is reputed that on one occasion Mathew Hopkins was responsible for the killing of no less than 19 women in a single day. He was both famed and feared for the pleasure and satisfaction he took in his work – so much so that, much later, his story was made into a classic horror film, with Vincent Price taking on the title role of Witch Finder General.

Before execution, those accused of witchcraft were brutally tortured. Their limbs were pulled from their sockets on the rack, their faces were pierced with the scold's bridle, their bodies were run through in the iron maiden, their fingers were broken in the vice, their nails were ripped out and their flesh was branded with red-hot pokers – until finally, almost mercifully, either the flames or the rope took them. Is it any wonder that false confessions were made to end such sickening tortures?

We must also remember that many of the people tried and executed for witchcraft were not even followers of the Old Religion and had no knowledge of nature deities or of Goddess worship. Many victims of the Burning Times were just ordinary, gentle people attempting to live quietly and peacefully in a dangerous and unpredictable age. Yet, like the wise women, cunning folk and other followers of the Craft, they too were condemned and killed on the charge of witchcraft.

By the late seventeenth century witchcraft appeared to have been stamped out, but in reality it had simply gone underground. However, the Witchcraft Act remained in force, revised and changed over time, for many years. It was in fact not fully revoked until 1951 – meaning that less than 60 years ago the practice of magic, the worship of the Goddess and the following of the Old Ways was still considered a criminal act.

The rebirth of witchcraft

For 300 years the Craft existed underground, hidden away like a secret society. Those covens that survived, usually made up of family members, continued to observe the sabbats of the Old Religion and to worship the Goddess as discreetly as possible. Rarely was anything written down, and old Books of Shadows (witches' magical diaries containing records of spells and rituals), though once regarded as prize possessions and family heirlooms, were hastily cast into the fire that the witch herself might be spared the flames or the rope. Ritual tools were left unadorned and were secreted among everyday objects so as to be unnoticable. Magical symbols were traced in the cool ashes of the fire and then quickly and thoroughly scattered after the ritual or spell was over so that any sign of witchcraft was erased.

In this way the Craft survived through a dangerous time. The seasonal Wheel of the Year was celebrated quietly but persistently, as were the esbat rites of the full moons. Spells, rituals and traditions were passed down through the generations by word of mouth. Everything had to be committed to memory, the older witches teaching the younger ones. Obviously, in this game of Chinese Whispers much was lost. Many of the spells and rituals that were not stamped out by the Witch Hunt were forgotten through the ages. What did survive, however, was expanded and built upon, and some of the rituals that had been lost were replaced with new ones. The essence of the tradition itself survived. Witchcraft remained, and slowly, tentatively, it began to re-emerge. But was the world ready for the witches yet?

During the Second World War, witches were allegedly very active, despite the fact that witchcraft was still against the law. Most of this activity involved working magically against Adolf Hitler (who was himself reputed to be using dark magic) and his forces. The swastika is actually an ancient magical symbol that stands for the creative and regenerative energies of the cosmos. But Hitler chose to reverse this symbol – a clear indication of negative magic at work – and use it to represent his own political agenda. British witches worked spells for rough seas to try to prevent the German ships landing on British shores and mixed 'go away' powders, which they threw into the ebbing tides to keep the German invaders away.

When the witchcraft laws were finally revoked in 1951, witches were free at last to practise their religion of choice without fear of retribution. A modern branch of witchcraft now emerged, known as Wicca. A key figure in this movement was Dr Gerald Gardner. He founded his own branch of Wicca, which became known as the Gardnerian Tradition. Together with his high priestess, Doreen Valiente, and his protégé, Raymond Buckland, Gardner helped to give witchcraft the credibility and respect it had so long deserved and been denied.

Gardner, Valiente and Buckland, and others like them, did much PR work for modern witchcraft. They helped to dispel the myths about witches, devil worship and black magic. But this work still is still going on today, with writers such as Cassandra Eason, Silver Ravenwolf, Fiona Horne, Titania Hardie and myself endeavouring to quell the fear and superstition that still lingers by being open about our lives as witches and empowered women of the twenty-first century.

The Burning Times are thankfully over, but they will never be forgotten. Witches today honour and respect the victims of the Witch Hunt, for without their unwilling sacrifice, we may not have achieved the freedom we enjoy today to practice our gentle, loving Craft openly and without fear.

The philosophy of the Craft

While witchcraft has a strong spiritual aspect that qualifies it as a religion, it is also a craft and an art. It is a path that leads us closer to divinity, yes, but it also gives us the freedom to work on our own personal development in our own way, rather than placing restrictions upon us as some more orthodox religions do. In witchcraft we can extend our minds; our beliefs and our strengths, fully embracing our personal power without breaking any religious rules. Witchcraft is an adaptable, self-affirming practice which teaches that it is up to the individual to discover and create their own path through life.

Does this mean that witchcraft has no rules? Absolutely not. Witches have guidelines to follow just like everybody else (see below). But the rules of the Craft are fairly simple, and they enhance our lives rather than restricting them or confining us to a set of outdated principles that may carry little weight in the reality of the modern world. Our code of ethics helps to create peace and balance in our lives. Everything a witch does, both within the magic circle and in her daily life, is done in the spirit of perfect love and perfect trust. Of course this is not always easy, but this is the ideal that witches try to live by, for to give out love and trust is to receive love and trust. When we deem others worthy of these gifts, we are also establishing and affirming our own right to have them.

Witches try to face life with a loving, trusting attitude and with the knowledge that our higher self will guide us along the path that is correct for us. Whatever we encounter on that path, even seemingly negative things, is for our greater good. This can be difficult to accept, especially when we are faced with illness, a bereavement, poverty or a bad relationship. Witchcraft won't save us from life's hard knocks, but it can make us strong enough to bear them and bounce back more quickly.

Generally speaking, witches are strong, independent individuals who choose to walk a higher path through life.

The ethics of the Craft

Perhaps the most important ethical guideline of the Craft is the Wiccan Rede. This is witchcraft's number one rule, and we try to keep it in our mind at all times. The Wiccan Rede states:

An' it harm none, do what ye will.

Simply put, this means that you must harm no other living creature, by either magical or mundane means. This also includes yourself, and witches endeavour not to harm themselves by abusing drugs, alcohol, food or sex. We take care of our bodies and honour them. We respect ourselves far too much to willingly indulge in any kind of self-harm or abuse.

A second important ethical guideline, the Threefold Law, gives another reason for harming none. The Threefold Law states that whatever we send out, either magically or mundanely, we will get back with three times the force and three times the consequences. The Law applies to both the good and the bad, so whether you send out kind, loving thoughts or nastiness and spite, this will be returned to you threefold in kind.

The Threefold Law explains why negative magic is a definite no-no, for if we send out a curse, we will be three times cursed ourselves. Witches do not hex or use their magical power to harm people in any way. If someone intentionally hurts us, we let the Threefold Law deal with them in its own way. Why get your magical hands dirty when the universal law will punish this person anyhow?

The closest a true witch ever gets to performing negative magic is a binding or banishing spell. Although such spells stand close to the fine line that separates the permissible from the unethical, in certain circumstances they are acceptable practice and are a useful tool when used correctly and performed with due care and attention. A binding spell is used to prevent an individual from doing harm to you and others, while a banishing spell is used to remove something or someone from your life.

Combining these two types of spell forms the strongest kind of protection magic there is. However, even such a well-intentioned ritual must be cast 'with harm to none'.

In other words, the spellcaster must state that the spell should work only if it is in the interests of the greatest good.

So when is it permissible to work such magic spells? In emergencies and as a last resort. If, for example, your teenage daughter is being stalked, it is permissible to banish the stalker from her presence with a spell. In this case you might also work a binding spell to prevent the stalker transferring his attentions onto another, less protected, young girl. It is important to note that all magic should be backed up by common sense and action in the mundane world. Thus you would also need to inform the police that your daughter was being harrassed. In taking this all-round approach, you will have created a shield of protection around your daughter – and hopefully ensured that the stalker gets the help he needs.

When practised ethically, binding and banishing spells allow a witch the opportunity actually to do something about an undesirable situation. If such spells are used in perfect love and perfect trust, they will quickly rectify the problem.

Personal power

Within each of us there is a spark of divinity, a tiny flame of magic. This spark is active whether you realise it or not, and unless you learn to control and direct it, it will determine your destiny on its own. Witchcraft can help you to connect with this divine force of personal power. As witches we acknowledge and accept our inner divinity, and we know that we are the creators of our own lives – we are all self-fulfilling prophecies.

This may be difficult to accept at first, particularly if your life seems to be less than you would wish it to be. But if you look closely and truthfully at your attitude to life, you will see that what you focus on is what you get. A positive attitude is therefore crucial. Witches are not dreamy by-standers waiting for their ambitions to be handed to them on a plate. A witch is a proactive participant in her own reality. She grasps life in both hands, moulds it to her liking using magic and personal power, and then lives it to the fullest! This power is within all of us. You have a tremendous force of personal power within you right now. Once you understand this, you will be able to shape your life to the unique pattern that you want. In this way you can discover and realise your ultimate destiny. So let's begin your magical training right now by discovering your very own personal power!

To evoke your personal power

The word evoke means 'to call forth'. In this case you are calling forth your own inner spark of magic.

◆ Go to a private place and sit quietly with your eyes closed. Take several deep relaxing breaths, breathing in through your nose for a count of four, holding your breath for a count of four and then slowly breathing out through your mouth for a count of four.

◆ Once you feel nicely relaxed, begin to repeat the following affirmation to yourself over and over again. Keep repeating it until you can feel its truth:

I am a powerful person. Power flows through me at all times. I am in total control of my life. I shape my own destiny. I am a witch and a powerful woman in my own right.

◆ Visualise a bright white light glowing all around you. This is your aura of power.

◆ Hold your hands about 2 cm (1 in) apart, palms facing each other. You should be able to feel a subtle magnetic force between your hands. Your palms may even tingle or grow warm. This is your own personal power. It is this force that is directed through magic and ritual. You can use this power in any positive way to change your life for the better.

Repeat this entire exercise on a daily basis until you feel fully attuned with your own personal power. In addition, repeat the following chant every morning on waking and every night before going to sleep:

I am power, I am power,
I am power.

Becoming a witch

So far we have looked at the origins of paganism, the history and philosophy of the Craft and the concept of personal power. But why would any modern woman seek to become a practising witch?

Well, perhaps it's because witchcraft offers women the chance to take control of their lives, bodies, minds and spirits. Or maybe it's because witchcraft honours women – all women, regardless of age, weight, size, colour, creed or sexuality. Perhaps it's because witchcraft honours a female deity, a goddess of many names and many talents and attributes. Or could it be that the practice of witchcraft actively empowers women in general and on a daily basis? I feel that the growing popularity of witchcraft is due to a combination of all these things.

Witchcraft is like a breath of fresh air sweeping across the modern Western world. After centuries of suppression in a patriarchal society, women are being attracted to witchcraft in droves; indeed, it is one of today's fastest-growing spiritualities. While we may still be living in what is predominantly a man's world, women are definitely coming into our own again.

Becoming a solitary witch isn't complicated. You won't need to locate a coven or adhere to someone else's ritual timetable. You won't have to go through lengthy group degree ceremonies or prove your magical ability to anyone except yourself. Because a solitary witch works alone, from her own home and garden (a way of working also known as hedge witching), hers is a most liberated form of witchcraft.

As a solitary, you will work your Craft in your own way and in your own time, slowly and methodically studying the art from books like this one and from the natural world around you. And you will fit your magic and rituals around your career, family and so on. You will create your own Book of Shadows too. And as you learn the Craft, you will be shaping your future, increasing your wisdom and empowering yourself as a woman on a daily basis.

The Triple Goddess

As a Maiden she carries the warm spring to earth;
As a Mother she gives the green summer its birth;
As a Crone she brings winter in — darkness and rest,
As the old and the weary she takes to her breast.
The Wheel turns, the Earth sleeps, yet the Goddess is here;
Though her voice has grown silent, we sense she is near.
And we wait as she waits, till the Wheel turns again,
For we know, like the moon, life must wax and must wane,
But all shall revive and all things will endure,
For the essence of life is immortal and pure,
As the Goddess herself is — not cruel and not kind,
With no sermon to preach to us, just one truth to find:
That the Wheel of Life will stop turning never
And that nothing is lost and Life goes on forever.

Aurora

The Goddess

It is thought that the Great Goddess is the oldest deity there is, and it has been estimated that she was worshipped for no less than 20,000 years, prior to the rise of male gods and the development of patriarchal society. For centuries the orthodox religions tried to stamp out the Goddess, and when they failed, they absorbed her into their spiritual teachings and adapted her to suit themselves. Thus the Great Goddess was sanitised, de-sexualised and stripped of much of her power, becoming little more than a token sidekick of patriarchy's all-powerful gods.

In this way the Great Goddess was broken down and given many alternative names – names that we still recognise and acknowledge today. In the Christian tradition there is Eve, for instance, who ate the forbidden apple from the Tree of Knowledge, thus bringing about the downfall of mankind through her 'original sin'; and Mary, the virgin mother of Jesus. In Greek myth there is Hera, long-suffering wife of the philandering, omnipotent Zeus; and Gaia, the Earth Goddess whose only apparent purpose is to be exploited for the sake of human greed. Such is the role of the Goddess within patriarchal religion.

As patriarchal religions grew in strength, the image of the Goddess gradually diminished and was eventually almost forgotten, while the women of the world were forbidden power, education and freedom, becoming the downtrodden, unpaid servants of their menfolk. In many societies women were considered to be property, being 'owned' first by their father or brother, and then by their husband. A remnant of this ownership survives in the traditional wedding ceremony, which contains the words, 'Who gives this woman to this man?', at which the father of the bride passes his daughter's hand into the keeping of the groom.

If we look back through the pages of history, it becomes apparent that as the Goddess was forgotten and replaced with the gods of the orthodox religions, life for womankind took something of a downturn. No longer honoured and revered as powerful individuals, women were dominated, suppressed and subjugated, and were denied many of the rights that men took for granted.

In Celtic times, when the Goddess was revered, land, property, wealth and the power that goes with those things were passed from mother to daughter. This custom was known as the Mother Right. But with the rise of patriarchal religions the Mother Right was forgotten and instead men took control of wealth, property and so on, with inheritance passing from father to son. Women were also denied the ancient right of Thigh Freedom, which was basically a woman's right to choose her own sexual partners and change them at will if she wished. This change of partner usually took place after a period of about seven years – and is perhaps the source of the modern concept of the seven-year itch! Under patriarchy, a woman's body was considered to be the property of her husband, to be used or abused as he saw fit. Gradually, all the power that women had held was slowly taken away from them, and men began to assume all the roles of authority in society.

This male-dominated world was the order of the day for hundreds of years, and it is only relatively recently that women have succeeded in taking back some of their power. Political campaigns such as the demand for female suffrage in the early twentieth century, and later the women's rights movement have brought women back onto a more equal footing with their male counterparts, while the creation of the contraceptive pill and the availability of condoms has once again allowed women the Thigh Freedom to choose their own sexual partners. And at the same time, a new awareness of the Goddess has been growing in both women and men, with Earth-based and Goddess-centred spiritualities gaining in popularity.

Western society today is on the brink of a great change as more people become disillusioned with the teachings of the orthodox religions and look towards alternative belief systems. This is a time when the Goddess is being reborn into society, and both women and men are welcoming her back into the world. But just who is this powerful feminine archetype and what relevance does she have for today's woman?

Who is the Goddess?

As we saw in the last chapter, pagans and witches believe that the divine energy, or life force of creation, is in fact both masculine and feminine (see page 12). This feminine energy is known to us simply as the Goddess, although she is called by many different names by many different people. Each witch will have her own perception of the Goddess, and there is no right or wrong way to view her; however, certain traits seem to be ever-present. For instance, it is generally accepted among witches that the Goddess is the personification of natural Earth and lunar energies. When we talk of invoking the Goddess, we mean that we are drawing upon particular energies associated with the natural world around us. This is one of the things that makes witchcraft so different from more orthodox religions. We do not see divinity as being out of reach; instead we acknowledge Her divine presence in all things – in the trees, in the moon, in the rocks and the earth, in fruits and vegetables, in the wind and rain, and so on. This effectively means that witchcraft is a spirituality that can be touched, tasted, seen, felt and heard. Rather than being beyond our reach, it is within our grasp on a daily basis.

Witches use the many faces of the Goddess to attune with specific energies and to seek assistance with particular types of magic. To those new to magic and witchcraft it may seem a little confusing that there are so many different goddesses, but if you imagine the Great Goddess as a huge multi-faceted diamond, and each individual goddess (Diana, Hecate, Gaia and so on) as one face of the diamond, then things become a little clearer. In this way we can see the meaning of the pagan phrase 'All goddesses are one goddess'. Let's now take a brief look at some of the goddesses most often associated with witchcraft. I have also mentioned, where appropriate, depictions of the individual goddess that you might like to look out for to decorate your altar space – more on altars later (see page 95).

Artemis

Artemis is the ancient Greek goddess of the moon and also of the hunt. Her Roman equivalent is Diana. Both were virgin goddesses, meaning that they were 'beholden to no man', which is the ancient definition of the word virgin.

Artemis is generally depicted carrying a bow and arrows, and is sometimes seen with a deer, a hound or a hare, all of which are her sacred animals. Occasionally, she is also associated with the cat. As a moon goddess, Artemis is strongly linked to witchcraft and has even been called the Goddess of Witches. She is also associated with the woods and wild places where the hunt might take place.

The powers of Artemis can be called upon to guide a new witch's first steps within the Craft. As she is a protector of all women, she can also be invoked to guard you against danger (especially from men) and to protect during childbirth.

Artistic depictions of this goddess are:

Diana by Briar

The Awakening Of Adonis by John William Waterhouse.

Gaia

Gaia is the Greek goddess of the Earth and fertility. She is the ultimate nature goddess, and as such she has found a new popularity in the green, eco-friendly movement. It is perhaps this goddess who has been most sorely missed, for as we have ignored her presence our world has fallen into a state of deforestation and pollution, resulting in the destruction of the eco-system and the ozone layer. We need to reconnect with Gaia if we are to right the many wrongs that have been done to the Earth. Gaia can be called upon to assist with any green issue, such as conservation, recycling and so on. She can help witches to attune with the sacred energies of Earth and the natural environment around them.

Any picture of the Earth or a globe can be used to represent Gaia.

Demeter and Persephone

Demeter, whose Roman name is Ceres, is the goddess of the summer and of the harvest. As such she is often depicted holding a sheaf of corn and poppies. She is the mother of Persephone (the Roman Prosperina), the goddess of spring and also of the Underworld. Theirs is a seasonal tale.

Persephone was abducted by Hades and taken down to his Underworld kingdom, where she was made queen. However, Demeter was so distraught at the loss of her daughter that the world became a barren place, and Zeus finally ordered that Persephone must return to her mother for six months of the year. Thus we enjoy spring and summer when Persephone and Demeter are together, and autumn and winter preside when Persephone once again returns to the Underworld.

Both these goddesses can be called upon to assist with mother/daughter issues. Demeter can be invoked for her gifts of abundance, while Persephone's powers can assist with asserting independence and dealing with unwanted masculine attentions.

Artistic depictions of this goddess are:

Prosperina by Dante Gabriel Rosetti.

Athena

Athena is the Greek goddess of wisdom, intellect and the arts. Her sacred animal is the owl, the bird of wisdom. She was a gifted spinner and weaver, and it was she who turned Arachne into a spider for daring to boast that she was a better needlewoman!

Like Artemis, Athena is a virgin goddess. She is also a war goddess and is usually depicted in full armour, wearing a helmet and bearing a spear and shield. She was known for teaching men to use their intellect together with the mental weapons of strategy and tactics in warfare, rather than brute force alone. Although never one to run from a fight, this goddess by no means advocates violence for its own sake, but she will support humanitarian wars which are for the greater good of all.

The powers of Athena can help modern women to attune with their inner warrior whenever faced with adversity. She can also help with any creative venture. She offers wisdom and clarity, together with a deep appreciation of the arts.

Any image of an owl or a female warrior can be used to represent this goddess.

Hecate

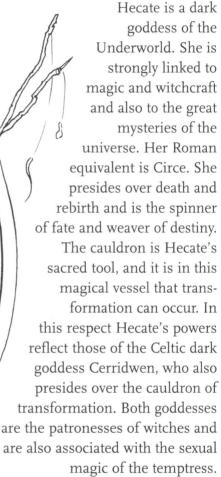

Hecate is a dark goddess of the Underworld. She is strongly linked to magic and witchcraft and also to the great mysteries of the universe. Her Roman equivalent is Circe. She presides over death and rebirth and is the spinner of fate and weaver of destiny. The cauldron is Hecate's sacred tool, and it is in this magical vessel that transformation can occur. In this respect Hecate's powers reflect those of the Celtic dark goddess Cerridwen, who also presides over the cauldron of transformation. Both goddesses are the patronesses of witches and are also associated with the sexual magic of the temptress.

Hecate was originally a goddess of the Amazons, and in this aspect she is often depicted riding a chariot pulled by dragons. Dragons are one of her sacred creatures, as are dogs, frogs, toads and serpents. She is also associated with three-way crossroads, and in the past offerings to her were left at such places. Other names that Hecate goes by are Queen of Witches and Queen of the Night.

Hecate is a powerful goddess and a mistress of magic and divination. She can be called upon for strong protection of any kind, but most especially against discrimination. She can help modern women come to terms with illness, bereavement and ageing, and she can be called upon to increase personal power, inner wisdom and magical ability. In short, Hecate is absolutely the goddess to attune with if you wish to become a skilled witch. She will nurture your power and protect you from harm.

Any image of a witch or cauldron can be used to represent Hecate. Alternatively ...

Artistic depictions of this goddess are:

Circe by Linda Garland

The Magic Circle by John William Waterhouse.

Aphrodite

Aphrodite is, of course, the Greek goddess of love and beauty. Her Roman counterpart is Venus, after whom Venice is named. Aphrodite was born from the foam of the sea, so sirens and mermaids are her hand maidens. The symbol of Aphrodite is the honeycomb, and pots of honey were once placed at her shrines as offerings. Tradition states that to place a pot of golden honey beneath the bed will encourage love-making and can give a flagging relationship a new lease of life! Honey bees, too, are sacred to this goddess, as is the rose, being the flower of true love. Frogs are also associated with Aphrodite, so linking her with the fairy-tale of the Frog Prince and the idea that to kiss a frog will bring your true love into your life.

As the goddess of love, Aphrodite is also strongly associated with sexuality, and you can call on her energies – and those of her hand maidens, the sirens – to increase your sexiness and allure, make you feel beautiful and desirable, and draw a new lover towards you if that is what you wish. But let's not forget that Aphrodite is the goddess of all love, not just the romantic variety, so working magically with her can enhance all your relationships.

Statues of this goddess make wonderful altar figures and are widely available from occult stores. They can also be found in holiday destinations in Greece and Italy.

Isis

Isis is one of the most powerful Egyptian goddesses, and she has come to represent all that is best about being a woman. She is a wife, a mother, a seductress and an enchantress, and mythology states that she performed the first form of mummification by embalming her husband, Osiris. She then used her vast knowledge of the magical arts to bring him back to life. Thus Isis is a goddess of birth, death and rebirth – a Triple Goddess in her own right.

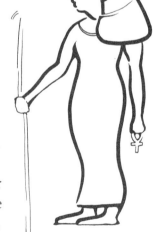

Her symbol is the serpent, which could be the reason why the Egyptian Queen Cleopatra used the bite of an asp to end her own life, thus thwarting the Romans. In choosing such a death she was reaffirming her native beliefs and attuning to her chosen goddess, Isis.

The powers of Isis can be invoked for any type of women's issue, for example motherhood, childbirth, widowhood, menopause and PMT. As a mistress of magic, Isis can also act as a spiritual guide and mentor on the magical path, particularly if you feel an affinity with Egypt or are interested in Egyptology.

Guinevere

It may come as a surprise to learn that witches view certain characters from Arthurian legend as aspects of the Witches' Goddess and God. But Celtic mythology and traditional British folkloric tales such as those of Robin Hood contain powerful archetypes. By attuning with them we can connect with our home soil and native heritage, so increasing our sense of belonging and enhancing our magical skills.

Guinevere stands for female independence and freedom of spirit. She is a love goddess and can also be seen as something of a seductress and femme fatale! Her relationship with Lancelot could be regarded as an affirmation of her right to Thigh Freedom, and she was strong-willed enough to have the courage of her convictions.

For modern women, Guinevere can increase a sense of inde-pendence and individuality. Attuning with her may help you to free your spirits from the demands of modern life and even inspire you to relieve yourself of an unhappy relationship or embark on a new one. This goddess will teach you first and foremost to be true to yourself, which is an important lesson that we must all learn at some point in our lives.

Morgan le Fay

Although Morgan le Fay is often portrayed as evil, she was originally a priestess of the Goddess and a follower of the Old Ways. When Arthur embraced the new Christian religion, Morgan felt that he had betrayed the Old Gods from whence his power and position had derived in the first place. In truth, King Arthur was the mythological link between the Old Religion and the new one of Christianity, and he made a valiant yet failed attempt to bring the two faiths together.

It is the Christian image of Morgan le Fay, as the evil sorceress, that survives today and that most people are familiar with. Was Morgan a sorceress? Almost certainly. Was she a mistress of the magical arts? Absolutely. There is no denying that Morgan's powers were great. Was she evil? Probably not. This is yet another instance of patriarchal scholars attempting to diminish the Goddess, turning her into an evil schemer who is the downfall of men. In fact, Morgan le Fay could be said to be the Arthurian parallel of the Biblical Eve.

I must admit, Morgan le Fay is my favourite goddess and it is from her that I took my own magical name, Morgana. Her name actually means Morgan the Faery, which hints at her pagan roots. The fact that she is the Queen of Avalon, the Celtic Otherworld, marks her as a priestess of the Great Goddess and the Old Religion. As Arthur's half-sister and the daughter of Queen Igraine, Morgan le Fay bears royal blood, and as the lover of Sir Accolon, a knight of the Round Table, she is assured a place within the court of Camelot. Just as Arthur is a Sun King, so Morgan le Fay is Queen of Winter and the dark season. The realm of night is her time.

This is a very powerful goddess who can be called upon for protection; justice and retribution; status; power; and the skills of enchanting, bewitching and seducing. She can also guide your steps on the magical path, but you must be whole-hearted in this and devote yourself entirely to the magical arts. This goddess has no patience for part-time Sunday witches. It's all or nothing with Morgan le Fay, so be certain that this is the path for you before you invoke her powers.

The Triple Goddess

Within witchcraft, the Great Goddess has three aspects. These relate to the three phases of the moon and the three phases of a woman's life. They are Maiden (new and waxing moon), Mother (full moon) and Crone (dark moon). All goddesses belong to one of these three moon aspects. For example, Hecate and Morgan le Fay are dark goddesses, so they fall into the category of Crone; Isis and Gaia are Mother goddesses; while Artemis, Persephone and Diana are all Maiden goddesses.

Collectively, the three aspects of Maiden, Mother and Crone are referred to as the Triple Goddess.

The Maiden

The Maiden is the first of the three aspects of the Triple Goddess. Hers is the new and waxing moon, the dawn and the season of spring. She stands for youth, freshness, births, new beginnings, seductions and enchantments. Her colour is white, symbolising innocence, purity and virginity.

The Mother

Next comes the Mother aspect of the Triple Goddess – and she is perhaps the aspect most frequently called upon. She is the abundance of summer and the first fruitfulness of autumn. The main part of the day and the full moon are her times of power. She is loving and nurturing and can offer gentle protection to those in need. She is creation, nature and Mother Earth. Her traditional colour is red, symbolising menstruation, birth and the blood of life.

The Crone

The final aspect of the Triple Goddess is the Crone, or Dark Mother. This is the goddess most feared by those outside the Craft with little understanding of Wiccan beliefs. The Crone is associated with death and the Otherworld/Underworld. Hers is the dusk and night, the waning and the dark of the moon, autumn's end and the depths of winter. Her colours are black and purple, which symbolise darkness, death and destruction, but also protection and deep rest. She is the stereotypical hag – old, bent, fearsome and enshrouded in a dark cloak. Yet she can also be the seductive enchantress – powerful, beautiful and strong – as we see in Morgan le Fay. However she appears, witches know that there is more to this goddess than meets the eye, for she is the keeper of the mysteries and the mistress of all magic. She is wisdom and release, old age and rebirth, divination and prophecy. She has a powerful association with life and death. She brings justice to wrong-doers in the form of karmic retribution. If you have need of her and can call on her without fear in your heart, she will provide powerful protection, for she is the guardian of witches and witchcraft.

As you can see, the Goddess is present in many ways and has many faces. This is one of the reasons why modern women are still drawn to her. There will always be an aspect of the Goddess that you can relate to, be it the feisty independence of a maiden goddess, the courage and valour of a warrior goddess, the nurturing love of a mother goddess, the flirtations of a love goddess or the seductive enchantments of a dark goddess. The Great  Goddess speaks to us on many levels, and if you listen closely, you will come to hear an inner voice that resonates with your own.

Finding your inner goddess

Most orthodox religions teach that divinity is outside the realm of human existence, that it is somehow above and beyond us. Of course, when the masses feel powerless, they are easier to control. As we've seen, however, witches have an entirely different way of thinking about divinity and relating to it. Witchcraft teaches that every living creature has a divine spark of magic within it. This is our life force, our own personal power. When we recognise this power, we are able to give it shape and form and maybe even a name. Perhaps this is the reason that witches choose their own magical name. When a witch says that she is in touch with her inner goddess, it is this personified power that she is talking about. This is not an egotistical statement. The most important goddess you will come to know is the one you hold within you. Because the Goddess and womankind are one, there is no separation, no great divide. The magic of the Goddess is in you right now, and you, my friend, are a goddess! This may be a little hard to digest, but if you didn't already feel the magic somewhere within you, you wouldn't be reading this book.

Okay, so there are days when the last thing you feel like is a goddess! Bad hair days, bad skin days, PMT days and those days of over-indulgence that have put you on the wrong side of your ideal dress size. We all feel that way sometimes. But getting in touch with your inner goddess can help you through those days and can put a skip in your step and a beam of confidence in your smile on any day of the week. This is because the Goddess teaches us that women do not need to conform to a Hollywood ideal to be beautiful. All women are beautiful, because they hold the power of the Great Goddess within them, and the Goddess is, after all, the epitome of feminine beauty and allure.

There is another more practical reason for attuning with your inner goddess, and that is that unless you connect with your personal power in this way, unless you learn to summon up your own inner magic, any spells that you cast will remain ineffective. So it is vital to your progress within the Craft that you accept and attune with your inner goddess. And after all, who wouldn't want to be a goddess? You already have that power within you. The remainder of this chapter offers ways in which you can connect with it, so that you can use your goddess power to improve your life.

The Goddess shrine

Creating a small space in your home dedicated to the Goddess is the first step to recognising your own inner goddess power. This space is known as a shrine, and it can be as subtle and discreet or as openly magical as you like. Creating a Goddess shrine will not only infuse your home with power but will also be a constant affirmation of feminine wisdom and magic, and may well become a source of comfort in troubled times. Your shrine will be like no-one else's, totally individual to you, and will grow and develop over time.

To begin with, you need to decide on the form your shrine will take. If you feel an affinity with a particular goddess, then your shrine could be centred on her alone. Alternatively, you could use different goddess images from various cultures, symbolising the multi-faceted Great Goddess. Or you could make the shrine quite abstract, using symbols of the Goddess such as sea shells and crescent moons, rather than figures of the goddesses themselves.

Next you need to decide where you want your shrine to be. A bedroom is a good place, or any quiet corner of the house where your shrine will not be disturbed. If you are creating your shrine for a particular goddess, choose a place that is suited to her energies. For example, a love goddess might be most powerful in the bedroom, a goddess of beauty in the bathroom, an abundant Earth goddess in the kitchen, and so on.

Once you have decided what kind of shrine you want and where, choose a central goddess image for it, such as a figurine or a picture to hang on the wall. Add to this a couple of white or silver candles in appropriate holders and burn incense here whenever you wish to attune with the divine feminine. You might also like to add fresh flowers, silk scarves (to be used as altar cloths), a round mirror to represent the moon, and anything you find with a crescent moon design. Take your time and have fun with this process. Experiment until you feel you have created a goddess shrine that works for you and your environment, and – most importantly – that makes you feel empowered!

Goddess blessing

This blessing is designed to be used on a daily basis, as you sit in quiet contemplation before your Goddess shrine. It will help you to connect with the universal feminine energies of the Great Goddess and, at the same time, to attune with your own feminine power. I suggest that you copy out the words of the blessing and keep it on your Goddess shrine.

When you perform this little ritual is up to you. I like to sit by my altar for a few moments each evening, but some people find that a Goddess blessing said first thing in the morning sets them up for the rest of the day. Choose whenever suits you best, taking into consideration what can be most easily incorporated into your own daily routine.

◆ Go to your Goddess shrine and light candles and incense. Spend a few moments sitting quietly and take several deep, calming breaths. When you feel ready, speak the following words, as you do so focusing on the feminine power you hold within you and the powers of the Great Goddess:

Gentle Lady, Mother of all, I come here in honour and in thanks. Thank you for all the wonderful things in my life right now and for all the wonderful things that are coming to me. Thank you for all the success I have enjoyed so far and for all the successes that are to come. Thank you for all the love and friendship I give and receive and for the protection you offer me and my family. I honour your divine presence in the natural world around me. May you continue to shower me with your gifts of love and abundance. So mote it be!

◆ Remain seated at your shrine for as long as you wish to, then blow out the candles and go about your day.

The cauldron of transformation

The cauldron is the sacred symbol of the Goddess and is a magical tool of transformation. You can incorporate this symbolism into your daily life by placing a small cauldron on your Goddess shrine. Full-sized cauldrons can be bought from occult stores, but they are quite expensive. In this ritual you can substitute any dark-coloured bowl, or even one of the small novelty cauldrons that are sold in most shops around Halloween.

◆ Place your chosen cauldron on your Goddess shrine.

◆ Whenever you have need of anything or are particularly grateful for something in your life, write it down on a slip of paper and place this in the cauldron. Leave it there until your wish has manifested or for three full lunar cycles if you are simply stating your gratitude for something.

◆ Repeat this ritual as often as required.

B A God S spell

This little spell was inspired by the mobile phone and the joy of text! It's a great little affirmation of goddess power and feminine wisdom. It can be called upon whenever you need a boost, or you can text it to a friend who is having a bad day.

◆ Tap the following text message into your mobile phone: 'B A God S!'

◆ Lock this message into your phone's memory so that you can call it up and read it to yourself whenever you need its power. No-one will ever guess you're making magic and attuning with your inner goddess! They'll just think you're on the phone!

Guinevere Dreams of Lancelot

Great knight in shining armour,
My champion and my love,
My defender and protector,
Our stars shine high above.
Striding through my thoughts,
Dancing in my dreams,
I see your golden hair,
Reflected in sunlight beams.
Lancelot, beloved,
My heart was always true.
All night and day my mind is lost,
Mulling over thoughts of you.
I hear echoes of your voice
Whispering my name;
I remember all we shared
And my heart is lost again.
Your eyes so icy blue,
As sharp as a jousting lance,
Could see into my soul,
Could render me entranced.
Your arms so strong yet gentle,
Clad in armour bright,
I feel them wrap around me
In the stillness of the night.
Always my protector,
Guarding me from strife ...
Then I wake to find the vision gone
Till you come back into my life.

Morgana

The God

You will probably already be familiar with the demonised version of the Witches' God that figures in Christianity. We have already seen how he came to be represented as evil by the early Christians and was transformed into their devil (see page 15). Fortunately, we live in a far less superstitious time, and people are generally more open-minded, but the idea that witches are devil-worshippers still prevails in some circles, and modern witches work hard to dispel this misconception.

Like the Goddess, the God is multi-faceted and is known by many names. He is the personification of the masculine energies of the universe, and his essence resides in every man – indeed, women have a small part of him too, in their masculine aspect. The God is associated with the sun and the heat of summer. The summer solstice (or longest day), when the sun's power is at its strongest, is his special time. The God is also seen in the might of the mountains, the vastness of the sky and the golden harvest that is cut down in sacrifice each year, only to grow again the following summer. He is the seed of all life, just as the Goddess is the mother of all life. They are opposites, yet they are also equal.

Perhaps the most popular image of the God is in a half-human, half-beast form, such as Pan, Herne, Cernunnos or the mythological centaur. In these aspects the God symbolises the interconnection of humans and animals, evincing that the animal kingdom is equal to the human race, not inferior to it, as many believe. In certain aspects the God is depicted with a pair of horns or antlers growing from his brow. This connects him to the animal kingdom and to the early God of the Hunt, who figures in cave paintings from Neolithic times. The curve of the antler or horn also symbolises the crescent moon, and thus the God's union with the Goddess.

The God is the protector of all animals, and he represents the wild force of vegetation and nature. He presides over sexual urges and procreation, and can be a powerful aid in increasing libido and sex drive. So when your man is feeling frisky, it could be that he is unconsciously attuning to his inner god! Working magically with one of the sexual aspects of the God, such as Pan, can help to improve your sex life, increase your passion or bring a new lover into your life. And just because the God is the essence of masculine energy that does not mean that he cannot be invoked by modern women – though if you choose to invoke Pan, expect a few surprises in the bedroom!

We will now take a look at some of the aspects of the God most closely associated with witchcraft.

The Green Man

The Green Man is the essence of the vegetative cycle of the year. He is the awesome power of the vast forest, the slightly spooky feel of the woods at night and the gift of the harvest waving in the fields. Most commonly depicted as a face made entirely of leaves, the Green Man can be found carved into old buildings and churches all over Britain. He is especially prevalent in rural areas, but he can be found in towns and cities too, especially where there are lots of old buildings. Many garden centres and pagan stores sell wall plaques fashioned to look like the leaf-faced Green Man, and these make beautiful centrepieces for a wall altar, or they can turn a quiet corner of the garden into a really magical place.

The Green Man has very protective energies, which is one of the reasons why he was carved into the stonework of old buildings. It is this protective energy that can make us feel a little uneasy when in dense woodland – the sun is shining, it's a beautiful day, but you feel as if someone is watching you through the trees, though you know nobody's there. This is the Green Man guarding his patch! There may also be a sense of connecting deeply with the Earth, as well as the adventurous feeling that anything at all can happen. Getting lost in the woods can be both an exhilarating and a frightening experience.

During the Middle Ages, the Green Man entered folklore in the form of Robin Hood. As the protector of Sherwood, Robin came to represent the outrage of the people over the new forestry laws set in place by the ruling Normans, which turned vast tracts of land into private hunting and sporting grounds for the Norman lords. Robin Hood's exploits in opposing and defying such laws might be viewed as the magical Green Man making his presence known. The fact that Robin took a wife, Maid Marian, further suggests that he is in fact an aspect of the Witches' God, with Marian being an aspect of the Goddess.

Other characters associated with the ancient Green Man are Jack in the Green, Puck in Shakespeare's *A Midsummer Night's Dream*, and the Green Knight of Arthurian legend. It seems that the Green Man will always be around, for his image has been used to draw attention to modern ecological and conservation issues – and who can forget the Jolly Green Giant from the TV ads?!

To modern witches the Green Man represents nature's ability to regenerate itself. He is the life-giving energy that enables our world to grow again and again. Seek the Green Man in your local park or beneath the trees in your own garden. Sit quietly or walk in silence and open your mind and spirit to his power. Let your feet take you where they will, for the Green Man will lead you into his enchanted realm and may show you some of his secrets – a bird's nest, a hidden spring, his face in the bark. Feel the strength and power of the Green Man and know that you have connected with the lord of the trees.

John Barleycorn

John Barleycorn is the sacrificial god of the harvest, and as such he is an important pagan deity among agricultural people. The yearly cycle of planting, growth and harvest illustrates the cyclical nature of life and the promise that from death new life springs forth. From wheat comes flour, and from flour bread, illustrating that death is only superficial and that the life essence merely changes form and shape. John Barleycorn personifies this endless renewal of corn and grain, and he is often seen in May Day and Midsummer parades in which men dress up in sheaves of wheat and straw to represent him. Each year John Barleycorn is cut down to feed and sustain the people, and each subsequent year he returns with another full crop, assuring us that the Earth is a place of complete abundance.

Herne the Hunter

Herne the hunter is a horned god who sports a magnificent pair of antlers on his brow. He is the protector of all wildlife, and the animal kingdom is sacred to him. Herne is usually depicted as a wild-looking man, with clothes made from skins and fabrics of various earthy hues. He is said to wear tiny bells, which are symbols of the Goddess and of his connection with her, and a magical tinkling sound accompanies him as he walks. Herne is also associated with the Otherworld and with the hunt. In this capacity he leads the Wild Hunt of winter, which is a pack of ghostly hounds and horses who come to collect the souls of the dead and take them on to the Otherworld. This hunt is said to be visible in black winter storm clouds and is most likely to be abroad on the night of 31 October, known to witches as Samhain.

Historically, Herne was said to have been a loyal huntsman who saved his king from the attack of a wounded stag. Legend states that

Herne placed himself between the stag and the king and was wounded by the stag's antlers. A magician pronounced that the only way to save Herne's life was to remove the stag's antlers and fix them to Herne's brow. This was done and Herne lived. However, his survival and recovery made the other huntsmen suspicious and envious of his new place as the king's favourite. Eventually, the king was persuaded to dismiss him, and Herne hanged himself from a tree in Windsor Great Park. His ghost is said to haunt the park to this day, most frequently being sighted in the area around a great oak tree that has come to be known as Herne's Oak.

It is likely that Herne the hunter is an amalgamation of various characters, in much the same way that Robin Hood and King Arthur are. In witchcraft his energies are invoked to assist with any kind of animal magic, such as calling a familiar or healing a pet. As an Otherworld god, he can also help us to come to terms with death and bereavement and our own mortality. Herne can also be invoked for protection of any kind.

Cernunnos

Cernunnos, whose name means 'the horned one', is another antlered god, this time originating with the ancient Celts. He is generally depicted sitting crossed-legged, wearing the torc of the Celtic people around his neck and often holding an antlered serpent. He is usually naked but is sometimes shown bearing the intricate patterns of Celtic tattoos.

Cernunnos has similar traits to Herne the Hunter in that he too is lord of the animal kingdom and keeper of the gates to the Otherworld. It could be that these aspects of Cernunnos were taken into the mythology of Herne or that these are different names for the same god in different areas of Britain. In general, though, Cernunnos is viewed as being somewhat wilder than Herne. While Herne has a quiet and gentle power, Cernunnos is more feral and untamed, probably due to his Celtic origins. The famous chalk figure of the Cerne Abbas Giant in Dorset, England, is thought by some to represent this ancient Celtic god. As he is a god of fertility, this would certainly tie in with the popular belief that to make love within the boundary of the Giant's chalk phallus will bring about the conception of a healthy child!

The image of Cernunnos can also be seen on the Gunderstrup Cauldron, a vessel thought to be of Celtic origin, which was found in a Danish bog in the 1930s. Cernunnos's association with the serpent links him to the Goddess and to the knowledge and wisdom of the Old Ways. Stags, dogs, rams and bulls were also especially sacred to him, although of course all animals were under his protection. It is thought that the Celts called upon the powers of Cernunnos to ensure the healthy procreation and survival of their livestock. He was also called upon to assist in any hunting activity. The energies of Cernunnos can be invoked by modern witches to aid in conception, to bring understanding of the animal kingdom and to attune with Celtic roots or ancestral heritage.

Pan

The Greek god Pan is perhaps the most notorious of the Old Gods. He is famed for his voracious sexual appetite, but there is far more to him than that. His Roman counterpart is called Faunus, a gentler, toned-down version of Pan. Both gods are depicted as having the upper body of a man and the legs, tail and cloven hooves of a goat. Both have curly hair and a beard, and little spiralled horns growing on their brow.

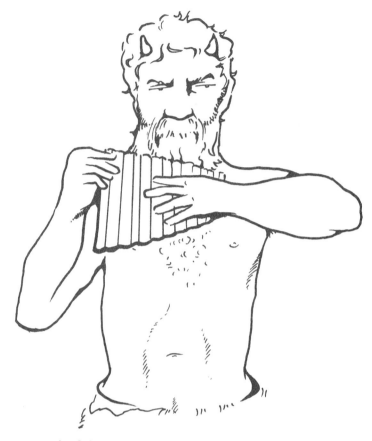

Pan is a playful god, a real party-goer! He is the original Lord of the Dance, and he adores music, playing his beloved pipes as he skips and capers in the woods. Working magically with Pan can increase the joy in your life, teaching you to take yourself and life in general a little less seriously. Be aware, however, that Pan is also something of a trickster, and he does like to have his little joke. In my experience, though, his jokes are always for the practitioner's highest good – he may encourage you to take a few risks, think outside the box or act in a way that is seemingly out of character for you. If you trust in the magic and go with the flow, you will have a lot of fun and may even learn a few things about yourself along the way.

It's almost impossible to work with this god and not feel the effects of his raw, sexual energy, for his is the most primeval and primitive of procreative energies. Of course, this can be useful if you are working to spice up a flagging love life, but if all you want is a skip in your step, you should be prepared for a few minor consequences! When Pan's energies are flowing through your life, you may find yourself in the middle of a fling before you know it, or that you are strangely attracted to someone whom you hadn't viewed in that way before. But one thing is almost certain, you will have the time of your life!

Yet Pan does have a darker side, for he can intimidate and frighten those who are insincere in their approach to magic and nature. It is from this god's name that the word 'panic' is derived.

Work with Pan if you wish to experience more joy and passion in life or if you are trying for a baby. He can fill your home with laughter, love, passion and fun, and he will always make you smile.

Cupid

We are probably all familiar with the popular image of Cupid as a chubby little baby. This image became very popular during the Romantic movement of the Victorian era, and is still very popular today, especially around St. Valentine's day. Originally, however, Cupid was a handsome youth, the son of Venus and therefore the god of love in his own right. His Greek counterpart was Eros, and both gods are depicted as beautiful young men, carrying a gilded bow and wearing a quiver full of arrows. These arrows had two functions; firstly they could make someone fall in love, and secondly they could make someone turn away from an unwanted or inappropriate love. Occasionally, Cupid is seen carrying a burning torch, with which he can inflame love in the hearts of men and women.

One myth tells of how Venus was jealous of a beautiful maiden called Psyche, and so she sent Cupid to work his magic and make Psyche fall in love with the ugliest man on earth. Cupid dutifully went off in search of Psyche, but when he found her, he fell in love with her himself! They began a clandestine affair, and Cupid would visit Psyche in the darkness of the night, telling her that she must never try to see his face or otherwise discover his identity. Unfortunately, curiosity got the better of Psyche, and she lit a lamp and looked on Cupid as he slept. Cupid awoke and left in a huff! Distraught, Psyche searched the world for her love god, until eventually Jupiter took pity on her and granted her the gift of immortality so that she and Cupid could finally be together for ever.

In view of all this, Cupid is a great god to call upon if there are obstacles lying in the way of you and a lover or if your love is for some reason forbidden. Invoking his energies can give a new depth to a superficial romance and can turn a fling into a long-term, committed relationship if that is what both parties wish for.

Odin

Odin, sometimes called Woden, is the main deity of the Norse pantheon. He is the one-eyed god of war and wisdom, of wind and rain, of divination and prophecy, death and rebirth. Odin's thirst for knowledge led him to sacrifice his eye: he gave it to the giant Mimir in exchange for being allowed to drink from the fountain of wisdom. In addition, Odin hung himself upside-down from the branches of Yggdrasil, the world tree, fasting for nine days and nights, until he learned the mysteries of death and rebirth. The Tarot card known as the Hanged Man represents this. It was during this shamanic experience that Odin had a vision of the runes and how they were to be used.

In witchcraft, Odin is still best known for his association with this tool of divination. The word 'rune' has its roots in *runa*, which means 'secret' – and the runes do reveal secrets to the diviner. As the very first master of the runes, Odin can be invoked to help you to understand this magical tool of divination. His energies are also useful if you wish to embark on a course of study or increase your knowledge in any way.

Thor

Thor is a magnificent warrior god of Norse mythology. He is the son of Odin and is usually depicted as the stereotypical Viking! He controls the powers of storm, thunder and lightening, and he is also associated with Battle Rage – a type of craziness that enables the warrior to fight to the end and not be put off by the scenes of carnage all around him.

Thor carries a battle hammer that is magically enchanted so that it always finds its mark and then returns to Thor's hand, in much the same way as a boomerang. The image of this magical hammer was carved into gravestones as a mark of protection for the soul, and small charms fashioned to look like a miniature version of Thor's hammer are still worn as a talisman of protection today, particularly by people who feel an affinity with Norse magic and mythology.

Thor can be called upon to lend the strength to face a particular challenge in life or for courage in adversity. He can help you to stand up for yourself and can assist modern women to rise above patriarchal rule and attune with their own warrior spirit, becoming strong and indomitable in their own right. Saying his name out loud three times is said to bring about a thunder storm.

King Arthur

Some pagans and witches who follow a Celtic tradition of magic choose to work their spells and rituals entirely around the Arthurian legends, and witches in general tend to view Arthur as an aspect of the solar god. As such, Arthur is associated with the sun and the summer months. Although the Arthurian myths have become greatly Christianised over time, if we just look beyond the superficial content and dig a little deeper, it becomes apparent that there is a strong pagan content hidden within them. The Round Table of Camelot's council chamber, for example, can be viewed as a representation of the moon, and the Grail (later Christianised as the drinking vessel of the Last Supper) has similar magical properties to the sacred cauldron of transformation. After his death Arthur was taken to Avalon by Vivienne, Guinevere and Morgan le Fay, who together represent the Triple Goddess. Arthur himself is a battle lord and is invoked by modern witches to lend courage and bravery. He can also be called upon if you are trying to find your true destiny.

Lancelot

Sir Lancelot was the greatest knight of the Round Table and the chosen champion of Queen Guinevere. The legends tell of their great love for one another, but there is more to this myth than meets the eye. Just as Arthur is associated with summer, so Lancelot is associated with winter, and this classic love triangle actually tells the story of the rivalry between the Summer King and the Winter King for the love of the Earth Goddess. This is a classic pagan theme illustrating the strong grip the seasons have on the natural world.

From a more feminist point of view, Lancelot offered Guinevere the freedom to be herself and gave her the courage and the strength of will needed to take back her power and her right of Thigh Freedom. The tale of Lancelot can thus teach us to be true to ourselves, regardless of what others think and to do whatever it takes to win our true love. Working with him can bring strength, courage and steadfastness.

Merlin

No chapter on the Witches' God would be complete without a look at the archetypal wizard, Merlin! Stories of Merlin are rooted in Welsh mythology, which states that he was born near Carmarthen in Wales. He was known as 'the wild man of the woods' (in this respect resembling Herne and Cernunnos), where he led a solitary life among the wildlife, engaging in shamanic activity. Merlin was the ultimate sorcerer, the master magician, and his knowledge extended to astronomy and cosmic divination, smithcraft, shape-shifting, illusion and prophecy, as well as general spellcraft.

The legend of Merlin is timeless. He reaches out through the mists of ages to modern magical practitioners everywhere. Indeed, he is a key figure in some traditions of witchcraft today. He is also the probable inspiration for such literary wizards as Gandalf, Saruman and even Albus Dumbledore!

Merlin's entire existence was enveloped in the strongest workings of magic; for this reason he can be called upon to help modern witches incorporate magic into their everyday lives. He can also teach us both to spin and to see through illusion, to look beyond the surface and perceive what lies beneath, and – perhaps most important of all – to question endlessly. Attuning with Merlin can help you to experience your own power and to realise your full potential as a witch, as well as to feel more self-confident in general. Like the goddess Hecate, Merlin can guide you on your first steps along the magical path, perhaps leading you to a particular type of magic you hadn't really considered before but which you find you have a natural aptitude for. On the whole, invoking the energies of Merlin will invite the power of magic to explode into your life with a very pleasant bang!

The God and modern women

As you can see, the Witches' God, like the Great Goddess, has many aspects, and it should be easy for you to discover one that you feel an affinity with. Many new witches struggle to come to terms with the pagan God, as he is so very different from the stern, judgmental God of Christianity and other more orthodox belief systems. It can be difficult at first to accept that the Witches' God is gentle, protective and fun-loving, as well as powerful, strong and slightly wild! Most witches go through this phase – I did myself. Don't worry. You will find the Old God in your own way and in your own time.

Getting to know the energies of the Witches' God in any of his many aspects will also give you a deeper appreciation of masculinity in general. It can be as tough to be a man as it is to be a woman, and people of each gender have to struggle with stereotypes and the various restrictions that society places upon them.

When we begin to welcome and understand the masculine energies of the universe via the pagan God, it can be easier to see the god in men. Just as you have an inner goddess, so men have an internal god form too. When you acknowledge this spark of divine magic within the men that you know, it can become easier to communicate and to understand the things they do. It may be that men and women will never truly and fully comprehend one another, but seeing the magic in each other helps. I believe that just as every woman is entitled to her PMT mood swings, so every man is entitled to his chest-beating moments! Bear this in mind next time your man gets confrontational.

Being a feminist, or fully empowered woman, is not the same as putting men down. We must learn to embrace our similarities and accept our gender differences without disparaging each other. Of course, this can be difficult when we are faced with a misogynistic chauvinist, but just take the high ground by telling yourself that such men only want to keep women 'in their place' because they are threatened by female power. Thankfully, such men are a dying breed anyway, and will one day be extinct, with modern men taking their place!

Attuning with the God

There are many ways in which you can get in touch with the masculine energies of the universe and the Witches' God. One way is to go to traditional summer parades and look out for representations of John Barleycorn or the Green Man. You could also search old buildings and churches to see if you can find the Green Man's face carved into the stonework. Walking through a large forest can help you to feel the energies of Herne and Cernunnos, and a visit to Sherwood Forest is a great way to connect with Robin Hood.

Mythology is also a useful tool. Read as much as you can about the gods of any culture that inspires you. The classical mythologies of Greece and Rome are great starting points. Or you might prefer to read the Arthurian legends, the folklore of Robin Hood, or the mythology of the Celts or the ancient Egyptians. Alternatively, try the creation mythologies of indigenous peoples such as the Native American Indians or the Aborigines.

You will be amazed at the similarities and parallels between mythologies from different sides of the globe, and you will probably discover which pantheon of gods and goddesses you can relate to best. There may be one particular aspect of the God that you come across again and again, and which holds a particular fascination for you. You may already have found him within this book, or he could be an old childhood hero, waiting to be rediscovered.

You might also like to read up on men's mysteries and masculine psychology. This can be a great way to understand the men in your life more fully and can make for deeper connections and more loving relationships.

The pagan God is a powerful source of comfort and strength for women as well as men, and he is waiting to welcome you into his world; to fill your life with love, fun and frolic; and to show you the way through his enchanted realms.

A shrine to the God

A good way to attune with the God on a daily basis is to set up a small shrine to him in your home. A simple statue or picture is enough if you want to keep the space small and understated. You could invest in a figure of Herne from an occult store, or perhaps buy a figure of an animal sacred to the god, such as a stag, lion, hound or bull. Alternatively, use a tea-light-holder with a sun design and burn tea-lights in it regularly. If you have more space, you could begin to collect the Green Man plaques and the Oak-leaf Man items that are sold in many gift shops and occult stores. Some stores sell candle-holders fashioned to look like a rack of antlers and designed to hang on a wall – this would make an interesting focal point for your magic. Items collected from nature, such as fallen leaves, acorns and pine cones, are also associated with the God and can be used to make a beautiful natural-looking shrine if cash is scarce.

There are many, many ways in which to create your shrine. The important thing is that it should be entirely individual to you. Once you have created this magical space, burn your chosen incense here regularly and spend time in contemplation of the pagan God and how you relate to him.

A God blessing

Performing a blessing spell to the God is a great way to attune with the masculine energies of the universe or to better understand your own masculine side and increase your own source of inner strength. It can also help you to empathise with the man in your life a little more and can open up the lines of communication between the two of you.

You can perform a God blessing any time you feel the need to attune with this pagan deity; however, you should always perform one on the summer solstice, the God's sacred and most powerful time. You may find it useful to copy the words of this blessing out and keep them on your shrine.

◆ Go to your shrine and light candles and incense. Sit for a few moments and concentrate on your breathing, taking deep, calming breaths.

◆ When you are ready, say the following words out loud or in your head:

Sky Father, Sun God, Green Man of the leaves, I come here in honour and in thanks. Thank you for the strength, protection and sense of purpose you give me daily. Thank you for the gifts of a free will and a strong spirit and for guiding me here to this path of the Old Ways. I ask that you grant me the wisdom to find my true life purpose, the courage to follow my heart wherever it may take me and the valour to be true to myself. I ask for the fearlessness to take risks and to have fun and frolic in the dance of life. I honour your presence in the natural world around me. May you continue to shower me with your gifts of courage, strength and mirth. Blessed be!

◆ Remain at your shrine for as long as you wish, contemplating the gifts of the pagan God. Then, when you feel ready, blow out the candles and go about your day.

Woman Wisdom

There is a strength deep in your heart
To help you when days are dark;
There is a knowledge deep in your mind.
To look is to find wisdom,
Woman's wisdom, burning bright,
Woman's wisdom creating light.
Woman's wisdom knows no bounds;
Woman's wisdom, a sacred sound.
There burns a fire that keeps you alive
Through all of life's woes and pains;
There is a valour that helps you through strife
And relieves your mind of strain.
Woman's wisdom is a guiding star;
Woman's wisdom will take you far.
Woman's wisdom is a friend so true,
For woman's wisdom lies within you.

Morgana

The Power
of Magic

Magic is real and spell-casting works. This may be hard to believe unless you already have personal experience of working magic. However, as any witch worth her wand will tell you, magic can and will make things happen!

People drawn to witchcraft tend to be open-minded about alternative therapies (such as aromatherapy and herbalism), tarot readings, astrology and so on. These are all different aspects of magic, so it may be that you have already floated in the shallows of the Craft for some time without being fully aware of it.

Before we begin to look closely at magic and witchcraft, we need to make one thing absolutely clear. When witches talk about magic they are not referring to the old rabbit in a hat trick or sawing someone in half! Nor are they alluding to card tricks or any other kind of stage theatricals. These all come under the heading of illusion, and while they are a great form of entertainment, they have nothing at all to do with witchcraft.

True magic is a force of nature, and working it is a skill that requires great discipline. It is also the aspect of the Craft that most people are initially drawn to. The spirituality of witchcraft usually comes later. Be honest with yourself for a moment and answer this question: did you pick up this book because you want to discover the Great Goddess, or because you want to learn how to perform magic and cast spells?

In general, people come to witchcraft because of the magic first of all, and there is nothing wrong with this. Everyone wants to improve their life in some way, and knowing how to work magic and cast effective spells is a powerful skill to have. And, of course, working with the universal energies of nature via magic draws us naturally towards the Goddess anyway. Nature is her realm, and true magic is an entirely natural practice, drawing on the energies of the Earth and the powers of the universe in general. So although in the beginning Goddess spirituality tends to come second to practical magic, eventually the two become one and sit comfortably together side by side. It is at this point that the dabbling ends and the real witchcraft begins.

What is magic?

At its most basic, magic is the gentle manipulation of natural energies in order to create positive change for the good of all. This may sound like a large and complicated task, but in reality magic and spell-casting can be as simple or as complex as the witch desires. Working any sort of positive magic introduces a witch to her inner power, and the more magic she makes, the greater her power becomes. It can be an exhilarating experience to cast an effective spell and to know that you have the power to influence and even change the environment in which you exist. And taking the time to perform magic rituals can help you to put some joy in your day and create a magical life for yourself.

The more you immerse yourself in the magical arts, the more skill you will develop and the more magic you will absorb, to the point where magic is in every aspect of your daily life and you yourself are magic! People will be drawn to you, though they won't be able to put their finger on why. Animals will trust you instinctively, and children and young people will be fascinated by you! This is what happens when you become a practising witch. You put a little joy into other people's lives by leaving a trail of positive magical energy in your wake.

Magic is a tangible energy, and even sceptical people pick up on it, though they won't be aware of what they're feeling and experiencing. Many people, however, still believe that magic is a supernatural force. This idea has been encouraged by movie-makers and writers of horror novels. In fact, nothing could be further from the truth. When working magic, a witch draws upon the energies of nature, in particular the elements of Earth, Air, Fire, Water and Akasha (the element of spirit). As such she uses only what are the building blocks of the natural world, so it stands to reason that magic is an entirely natural practice, no more supernatural than the sudden appearance of a rainbow!

For witches, magic is a way to take charge of your life and mould it to your liking. They prefer not to put the blame for things they don't like about their life on the past, their parents, their poor education, boredom and so on. They accept personal responsibility for their lives and endeavour to take full, independent control of them – as much as is humanly possible. Of course, there are things that even witches cannot change, such as terminal illness, drunk drivers, war, terrorist attacks, natural disasters and so on. But for everything else there's magic!

ɦow magic works

When you begin to work magic, you begin to alter your reality. The very first effective spell you cast will alter your future to some degree and a change will come to pass. How big a change depends on the purpose, focus and magical intent of the spell. But just as throwing a pebble into a lake causes a succession of ripples to expand across the surface of the water, so even the smallest spell will create ripples within the fabric of your life. This is why in witchcraft there is so much emphasis on personal responsibility and the 'an' it harm none' rule (see page 21). In working magic you are altering your own personal reality and so causing a knock-on effect within the greater tapestry of life.

We have said that witches work with the natural energies around them, but this alone is not enough to create an effective, life-enhancing spell. It is also necessary to evoke your own inner magic and fully believe in your power as a witch. You do this by attuning with your internal source of personal power and acknowledging its presence within you. Witches also carefully choose the appropriate tools of nature for their spells. This is where such things as crystals, herbs, oils, incense, sea shells and so on come into play. In this way you can weave together your own internal power and the power of nature. Thus the seed of magic is sown. Even so, unless the witch is totally dedicated and focused on her magical working, the spell will remain ineffective.

Absolutely anyone can cast a spell, but it takes a special kind of person to cast an effective spell. This is why so many people new to witchcraft fail in their first attempts at spell-casting. Either they weren't dedicated to and positive about their goal, or their attention wavered and they became distracted while casting the spell.

Willpower has a big part to play too. The most powerful witches tend to be very strong-willed individuals. They are determined and resourceful, and – like a dog with a bone – they don't give up easily. If one thing doesn't work, they change their approach and try something else. Persistence is one of the most valuable qualities you can have, as it virtually guarantees eventual success. And this is true in magic too. It takes time, effort and dedication to learn the magical arts to any level of competence, but once mastered, magic is a skill you will have for life, one which no-one can take away from you.

The components of spell-casting

As with any other skill, magic can be broken down into specific components that together serve to make spells effective and powerful. They are as follows:

1. Need
2. Emotional attachment to the goal
3. Knowledge
4. Belief
5. Visualisation and affirmation
6. Willpower
7. Release
8. Emotional detachment from the spell
9. Trust

Need

First off, you must actually need what you are casting for. This means that the ultimate goal of your spell must be for your highest good – to enhance or expand your life path in some way. A spell for a new love will only be effective if you need a new love in your life right now. If you are still emotionally damaged from a previous relationship, it is unlikely that the spell will work, as your first need is time to heal. The same is true of money spells. Ask for only as much as you need and maybe a little more for comfort's sake, but don't ask for £1 million and expect the spell to work. Need, not greed, is the foundation for effective magic.

Emotional attachment to the goal

You must be truly dedicated to your magical goal. You must want what you are casting for, and – more importantly – you must be able to see yourself having it. If you can't honestly see yourself passing a driving test and zipping around in your own car, then any spell you cast to make this happen will probably remain ineffective, because your emotions are not linked with the goal. Throughout the casting of the spell you must be able to feel the joy your goal will bring you. Simply put, if your heart isn't in it, the spell won't work.

Knowledge

This is knowledge of the magical arts. What kind of spell to cast, when to cast it, what tools to use, what words to say and so on. Of course, this knowledge will only really come with practice, but books like this one can teach you the mechanics of spell-casting and the basics of magical knowledge. You will learn more as you gain in experience. And even truly adept witches are still learning their craft, because magic is unlimited, so there is always something new to learn and a new depth of knowledge to be attained.

Belief

To work effective magic, you must be absolutely convinced that you have the power to change things. You must believe in yourself, in your magic, in your goal and in the spell itself. This is the area where new witches often trip up, as they imagine that if they light a candle and read a few words out loud, magic will happen. It won't. You are the magic, and you must believe in yourself and your power as a witch if you want your spell to manifest and bring your magical goal into being.

Visualisation and affirmation

These are the two key tools of all effective spell-casting. Visualisation is probably the the most important aspect of any spell. You must be able to focus on your goal and see the desired effect clearly in your mind's eye if you are to manifest it. This is the main driving force of magic. The more detail you give your magical visualisation, the more chance you have of casting a spell that works. An active imagination is a great help to a witch as it enables her to visualise in depth the goal she is trying to bring into being. You should hold the visualisation throughout the spell. Focus on your goal and imagine it as if it has already happened – you have already passed your driving test and the examiner is shaking your hand. Try not to let your thoughts wander or allow yourself to be distracted. This may be difficult at first, but it will become easier the more you practise.

There is nothing mysterious about visualisation. It is something we all do quite naturally on a daily basis, for instance when we picture the face of the person we are speaking to on the phone. All we are doing when we cast a spell is honing this natural skill and utilising it to the most powerful effect.

Affirmations are key components of spell-casting, too. An affirmation is a positive statement that is generally repeated a number of times (usually three, six or nine). In magic, affirmations usually take the form of chants or charms, and making use of this technique is called 'speaking the spell'. Affirmations can also be written down as part of the spell and then either burnt, buried or carried by the witch as a link to the magic.

Another form of affirmation is the practical action that is carried out after the spell. This is sometimes referred to as backing up the spell in the mundane world, and all magic is supported in this way. For instance, if you cast for a new job, you need to back up the spell by filling in application forms and going to interviews. This is known as an affirmation of action, and it links your magic to your everyday life. This kind of affirmation is an intrinsic part of spell-casting. Failure to follow through in this way may well result in the failure of your spell.

Willpower

Anything worth doing takes willpower, and magic is certainly no different. In spell-casting it is willpower that brings about the desired outcome. You simply focus on your visualisation and will it to happen, and then you do everything humanly possible to make your spell work. This technique is behind the final sentence of many spells: 'This is my will. So mote it be!', meaning this is what I want, and it must happen because I am giving it no other choice. Some people imagine that they don't have any willpower, but this is really not the case. Without exception we all have willpower. Their problem is that they do not tap into their willpower and use it effectively. Everybody has free will. Using your willpower is a matter of directing that free will constructively towards a positive end. Magic is a powerful way to do this.

Release

Once you have worked your way through the spell, you need to release the magical power you have raised. Only when you release the magic you have conjured can it move out into the universe and do its work. There are several ways to release the power. You might allow a spell candle to burn down, releasing the magic gradually. You might burn a written affirmation or spell paper, or bury it in the earth. You might release a balloon, untie knots in a cord, burn incense or point a wand or athame (ritual knife) up into the sky. If you are using a spell from a book, it will give detailed instructions on how to release the power. When you begin to write your own spells, however, you will need to choose an appropriate method for yourself and incorporate it into the casting.

After the spell, the witch must also release any magical power that is still lingering about her person. This is known as grounding. One method of grounding is to lie down on the floor. The witch will then eat and drink something to complete the grounding and rebalance her own internal energies (as working magic can be an energy-sapping business). This practice is probably behind the tradition of the ritual feast, known to witches as 'cakes and ale'.

Emotional detachment from the spell
As we have seen, emotional involvement in the spell is vital to its success. If your heart isn't in it, then the spell simply won't work. But at this stage in the proceedings it is equally important to let the spell go. You have released the power of your magical working, and you must now detach yourself from the spell on an emotional level or you will inadvertently hold your magic back and prevent it from being successful.

This is often a difficult skill for a new witch to learn. If you put your heart and soul into something, the last thing you want to do is let it go and not give it another thought. But that is exactly what you must do if you want your spell to work. Once you have released the power and grounded yourself properly, try not to think about the spell at all if you can help it. Don't sit there wondering when it will happen, how it will happen or if it will happen. Just don't think about it. This may take a lot of discipline, but what you most need to do now is back your spell up with actions in the mundane world and be patient.

Trust
If detaching from a spell is difficult, then having complete faith and trust that it will work is even harder. Still, I never said being a witch was easy! The final stage of any spell is trust: trust in yourself that you did the best you could in that moment, trust in the universal

powers of abundance (life doesn't have to be a constant struggle), and trust in the powers that be – that whatever the outcome of the spell, it will be for your highest good. Remember the witches' saying, 'in perfect love and perfect trust'.

All of the above components must be present in order for a spell to be effective, so it is easy to see why many new witches fail in their first attempts at magic. There is a lot more to spell-casting than meets the eye.

Be aware, too, that magic can be unpredictable – even if you are an adept witch. It often forces us to look at things in a different way and think outside the box. For example, some years ago, when I was struggling to make a living as a writer, I cast a spell to help me find a 'rent job' – meaning a source of part-time employment that would better enable me to meet my living expenses. I was suddenly drawn to sign up with a temping agency, which is not something I'd ever really considered before. A couple of days later I began a temporary placement with the local council, as a cashier taking people's rent! The placement lasted just long enough for me to pull in more writing work and meet my immediate financial demands.

One final point to be made with regard to spell-casting is that you must be specific. Don't leave your spells open to interpretation; otherwise they may work, but not in the way you envisioned. Or you may not get what you wanted but what you asked for! So if you want a passionate love affair, don't spell for a 'companion' or you could end up with a puppy! Be very clear about what you are casting for. If you follow the tips above, you won't go far wrong.

Types of magic

There are a wide variety of spells around, some of which have been passed down through time, others of which make use of ultra-modern objects such as a mobile phone or a paper clip. Spells have been a part of all cultures the world over, and they have been present in one way or another through all the ages of history. But while the vast array of spells available to the modern witch verges on the mind-boggling, the spells themselves can be categorised into a small number of types of magic. The following are some of the most popular ones.

Sympathetic magic

Sympathetic magic works on the basis that like attracts like. It usually incorporates some kind of link with the subject of the spell – for example a lock of their hair, a sample of their handwriting or an item that once belonged to them – or with the desired outcome – for example the written address of a home you want to buy or a picture of a holiday destination you wish to visit.

The best known branch of sympathetic magic involves using a poppet. A poppet is a doll, usually fashioned from fabric or wax, which is used to represent a person. This doll is stuffed with herbs appropriate to the goal, and some form of personal tag, such as a lock of hair, is added to provide the link. The doll is then used to bring about the desired magical outcome. For example, it could be bound to another doll with a red ribbon to incite love, or it could be anointed with healing oils to heal the subject. Occasionally, such poppets are stuck with pins. While much has been made of this technique by movie-makers, there is actually no evil intent behind it. On the contrary, pins are generally used to prick someone's conscience (or their heart), to release past pain or current illness, or to bring down a swelling or inflammation. In all of these spells, the purpose is to work magic for the good of all and with harm to none.

Petition magic

Petition spells are one of the easiest types of magic to perform. In fact, there is a good chance that you have performed this type of magic already without even being aware of it. Petition magic is simply the act of writing your magical goal or request on paper – so all those letters you wrote to Santa in the past actually had a magical foundation! Petition magic has also been incorporated into the everyday lives of regular church-goers, who are often invited to write their particular wish or prayer on a slip of paper and leave it in a special box near the altar.

In witchcraft, the petition paper is usually burnt or buried to release its power, although it may alternatively be hung on a branch, placed inside a balloon and let go of, or folded into a paper boat and floated away on a stream (particularly if petition magic has been used in conjunction with elemental magic).

Elemental magic

In this type of magic the elements are used as a focus – and in fact almost all spells use elemental magic to some degree. Earth, Air, Fire, Water and the fifth element of Akasha (or spirit) are generally represented in some way on the witch's altar, and each one is linked to certain aspects of magic, as follows:

Earth
- Stability
- Fertility
- Abundance
- Prosperity
- Growth
- Home life
- Family and friends
- Familiars

Air
- Communication
- Concentration
- Inspiration
- Creativity
- Joy
- Laughter
- Happiness
- Developing talents

Fire
- Love
- Sex
- Passion
- Power
- Protection
- Desirability
- Courage
- Valour
- Strength

Water
- Healing and health

- Tranquillity
- Dreams
- Wisdom
- Divination
- Psychic development

Akasha
- Spirituality
- Transcendence
- Protection
- Guidance
- Power
- Knowledge

Element magic takes us back to our natural roots, putting us in touch with a simpler time when magic was an accepted part of society and people's lives were governed by nature. In using natural tools such as gems, crystals, pebbles, fallen leaves, twigs, feathers, plants, sea shells and so on, we are drawing upon the particular energies of their associated element and of the elemental being that rules over that aspect of nature.

Elementals
Elementals (also known as faeries) preside over the natural cycles of our world. Each element except for Akasha has its own elementals. The main elemental for each element is as follows:
- Earth – gnomes
- Air – sylphs
- Fire – salamanders
- Water – undines

Knot magic

This is another very simple form of spell-casting, in which knots are tied into a length of ribbon, cord, rope or fabric while the spell-caster focuses on and chants the magical intent. One traditional form of knot magic was once used by sailors, who would ask a witch or wise woman for a length of knotted rope to control the weather at sea. To undo one knot would bring a slight breeze; to undo two knots would invoke a good strong wind, just right for sailing a ship. The third knot should never be undone at sea, as this would cause a terrible storm.

Divination

Divination is the art of fortune-telling and foresight. There are many branches to this kind of magic, including astrology; the use of oracles such as the Tarot cards or rune stones; dowsing with a pendulum; scrying (looking into a crystal ball, magic mirror or a pool of water); and the gifts of premonition and prophetic dreaming. It is likely that you will already have indulged in some form of divination, if not as a practitioner then as the receiver of a reading. Any form of divination takes time and practice to learn, but divining is a valuable skill and should be a part of your training in the magical arts. Choose whichever method most appeals to you, invest in the appropriate tools and start learning how to use them. Remember that such a skill cannot be learned overnight, but be patient and eventually your efforts will be richly rewarded.

Candle magic

Candle magic is very popular with both new witches and experienced practitioners alike. Because it is so simple, though, many people forget to visualise and focus properly – and then they wonder why their spell didn't work. Straightforward as candle magic may be, it still requires a high degree of imput from you if your spell is to be effective! Candle magic can be used alone or it can form a part of a larger ritual. It is also a branch of elemental magic, being a type of fire spell. Careful choice of the candle is essential, as the colour holds a magical power all of its own (see below). If you are interested in this form of spell-casting, which is perfect for neophyte witches, read my book *Candleburning Rituals,* which explains this type of magic in depth and has lots of spells for you to try.

Colour magic

In magic, each colour has a set of associations and can thus be used to add appropriate energies to a spell. I mentioned coloured candles above, but colour magic can also take the form of incorporating balloons, ribbons, inks, crystals, flowers and so on in a spell. The following is a list of colours and their magical meanings:

◆ Silver – femininity, moon power, the night
◆ White – purity, cleansing, childhood, innocence, truth, protection
◆ Gold – masculinity, sun power, the daylight hours
◆ Yellow – communication, creativity, clarity, exams and tests
◆ Green – finance, security, prosperity, employment, career, fertility, luck
◆ Light blue – calmness, tranquillity, patience, under-standing, good health
◆ Blue – healing, wisdom, knowledge, dream magic
◆ Pink – honour, friendship, virtue, morality, contentment, self-love
◆ Purple – power, mild banishings, psychic ability, ambitions, inner strength, nobility

- ◆ Orange – adaptability, zest for life, energy, imagination, social skills
- ◆ Brown – neutrality, stability, strength, grace, decision-making, pets, family issues
- ◆ Red – love, attraction, power, passion, virility, ardour, courage in adversity
- ◆ Grey – cancellations, reversals, anger, greed, envy
- ◆ Black – strong banishings, bindings, limitations, loss, grief, confusion, defining boundaries, strong protection

Magical correspondences

A magical correspondence is any item used in a spell in order to strengthen and empower it. This includes herbs, trees, stones, colours, crystals, oils and incenses, directions, elements and elementals. Below is a list of correspondences relating to the three most popular areas of magic. When you begin to create your own spells, you can use this chart to choose appropriate correspondences to make your working powerful and effective.

Correspondences for love and passion
- ◆ Element – Fire
- ◆ Elemental – salamander
- ◆ Herbs – apple, cinnamon, clove, coriander, gardenia, ginger, jasmine, patchouli, rose, violet, ylang ylang
- ◆ Trees – apple, elm, sycamore, maple
- ◆ Oils – clove, jasmine, patchouli, rose, ylang ylang, lavender
- ◆ Crystals – amethyst, rose quartz, carnelian, jasper

Correspondences for success and prosperity

- ◆ Elements – Earth and Air
- ◆ Elementals – gnomes and sylphs
- ◆ Herbs – mint, tea, bayberry, almond, cinnamon, patchouli
- ◆ Trees – fir, pine, beech, oak
- ◆ Oils – peppermint, bayberry, patchouli, almond
- ◆ Crystals – aventurine, jade, peridot, iron pyrites (fool's gold) loadstone, magnets

Correspondences for power and protection

- ◆ Element – all
- ◆ Elemental – all
- ◆ Herbs – basil, bergamot, carnation, eucalyptus, lavender, rue, nutmeg
- ◆ Trees – ivy, poplar, blackthorn, yew, oak, holly, hawthorn
- ◆ Oils – eucalyptus, lavender, rose geranium
- ◆ Crystals – tiger's eye, sodalite, azurite, blue lace agate, clear quartz, smoky quartz, obsidian

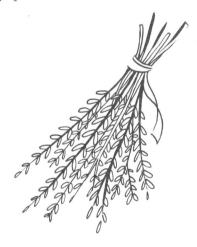

Virgin

I am a Virgin; I need no other.
I am a Virgin; I refuse to be smothered.
I am a Virgin in the ancient sense.
I am a Virgin; I am my own defence.
I am a Virgin, owned by no man.
I am a Virgin; I am what I am.
I am a Virgin, fragile but not weak.
I am a Virgin, with an independent streak.
I am a Virgin; unclipped are my wings.
I am a Virgin; I experience all things.
I am a Virgin; I may choose to make love.
I am a Virgin; I am as pure as the dove.
I am a Virgin, delicate yet strong.
I am a Virgin; I know where I belong.
I am a Virgin; to myself I am true.
I am a Virgin; I will always win through.
I am a Virgin, needing no-one but me.
I am a Virgin; I will always be free!

Morgana

Magical Tools

Witches use a variety of tools as a way of connecting with their inner magic and focusing on their magical intent. Tools are both practical and symbolic devices, the symbolism helping the witch to attune with the magic and power of the universal energies. In gathering together her tools and setting up an altar, the witch is affirming her intention to make magic and to take charge of her life using spell-casting. This is why the tools and altar of a witch simply ooze magic and power. They are not just a collection of decorative objects, although many Wiccan tools are beautifully crafted, but they are also a source of power and a symbol of independence, control and personal belief. Nevertheless, it must be said that tools are not essential. A powerful witch can cast a spell with no tools at all, just by focusing on her intent and willing it to happen. But tools can act as a kickstart to your brain when you want to make magic. And, of course, finding and buying your tools is a fun experience in itself – especially if you like a bit of retail therapy!

However, it is not necessary to have a lot of money at your disposal to come up with a set of tools. Most witches start out with tools that are home-made or have been adapted from regular household items. As you will see, most witches' tools can be found in the kitchen, so there is no need to wait until you have acquired a pewter goblet, a cast-iron cauldron and a custom-made athame before you cast a spell. Although there is something quite enchanting about an altar set up with beautiful Wiccan tools, such custom-made items are very expensive to buy, and it will probably take you a while to build up a complete set.

Although you don't need to worry about collecting a full set of crafted tools all at once, you do need to keep your tools – home-made or adapted – for magical purposes only. Even if your athame is an old kitchen knife, it is a sacred object and should be kept solely for ritual. It should not be used to chop vegetables with! If you keep your tools (regardless of their origin) separate from your daily life, they will come to represent your magical life, and you will begin to feel the power of witchcraft as soon as you pick them up to use them or to set up your altar. They will also come to represent your chosen spiritual path, your dedication to the Old Ways and your practice of the Craft.

Magical tools can be divided into three groups: those that are used in rituals and on the altar, those that are used for divination and those consumable items, such as candles and incense, that form an intrinsic part of spell-casting.

Ritual tools

Ritual tools are items that are used to create a formal altar set-up, such as the wand, the chalice, the pentacle and so on. These items are the staples of the Craft and they serve to pull all the elements of a spell working together. Each of the ritual tools represents one of the elements and so is linked with the powers associated with that element. For example, the pentacle represents Earth and all Earth energies. It is therefore invaluable in spells cast to attract wealth and prosperity. All the ritual tools should be present on the altar and will play some part in most spell-castings. Below is a basic description of each major ritual tool and its purpose within the Craft.

Athame

The athame is the witch's ritual dagger or knife. It is never used to cut anything; therefore its blade is dull or blunted. Traditionally, it should have a black handle and a double-edged blade, although today new athames are being created in designs that do not conform to this tradition. Swords, a paper knife and kriss blades also put in regular appearances on my own altar. A basic kitchen knife can be used until you find your athame – but remember not to use it for anything else. The athame represents the element of Fire and the powers of strength and protection. It is used to direct energy and to cast the magic circle. It should be placed in the southern quarter of your altar, the direction of Fire.

Sword

As first cousin to the athame, the sword is used by many witches to direct power and cast the circle. Although they are expensive to buy, swords simply ooze magic and enchantment, and many occult stores sell swords specifically created for the purposes of ritual and magic. Although some people shy away from the idea of owning a sword, with its connotations of war and bloodshed, for me the sword represents strength, honour, valour, courage in adversity and Celtic magic. If you like the idea of having a sword, you can use it interchangeably with, or even instead of, the athame. Both have the same magical associations.

Wand

When people think of magic, the first thing that usually comes to mind is the magic wand. And witches do use wands, although we don't leave a trail of stars and sparks in our wake when we wave them, more's the pity! In witchcraft, the wand is used to represent Air and also to direct energy, in a similar way to the athame. The power of the wand, however, is more gentle, and it is often used to direct energy straight into an object. Perhaps this is where we get the story-book image of a witch tapping an object three times with her wand in order to magically enchant it. In fact, a witch uses a wand to help her focus her own magical energy into an object, projecting her power through the wand.

Magical wands can be made of wood or crystal. A wooden wand is by far the simplest and least expensive to obtain, and is usually the first tool that a witch comes by, as it can easily be a length of fallen twig discovered while out walking. Of course, ritual wands are also available from occult stores, made from various woods strongly associated with magic, such as hazel, willow, yew, holly and oak. Such wands can be bought plain or carved with runes and magical sigils, and strung with feathers, gems and beads. Crystal wands are generally made from polished obsidian, clear quartz, rose quartz or amethyst. These are beautiful tools but they can be quite expensive and may be beyond the means of a new practitioner who is still deciding whether or not the Craft is the path for them.

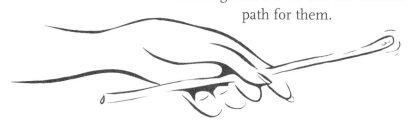

It may be wisest in the beginning to obtain your wand from a generous woodland. If at all possible, try to wait until autumn, when the trees are naturally shedding their dead wood. I am not an advocate of cutting wands or staffs from living trees, as I feel it is unnecessary vandalism when lots of twigs fall naturally. A wooden wand is a great way to connect with the strength and power of trees.

Traditionally, a wand should reach from your inner elbow to the tip of your middle finger. Your wand should be placed in the eastern quarter of your altar, the direction of Air.

Pentacle

The pentacle is arguably the witch's most important tool. It is a flat disk with a pentagram, or five-pointed star, inscribed upon it, and it is used to charge items such as candles, crystals, gems, jewellery, charms, spell pouches and papers, and so on – that is, to instil them with magical power and energy while the spell is being cast. The pentacle represents Earth, and it sits in the centre of the altar, slightly towards the northern quarter (the direction of Earth). You can make a pentacle from card, clay or wood, or you can buy one from an occult store. This is an essential tool, as many spells make use of its power.

Some witches, myself included, also choose to wear a silver pentacle necklace as a reminder of their magical path and spiritual belief system. This is much more than a fashion statement. Silver is the metal of the goddess, and the pentagram is one of her symbols. In wearing the pentacle, the witch is declaring her reverence for the Goddess and the Old Ways. It is also a great visual reminder of the magic you carry within you. I never take off my pentacle necklace, and it has become a treasured possession. Take a look in any New Age or occult shop and you will probably find a wide range of pentacle jewellery to choose from, so you should be able to find something that suits you and your budget.

Chalice

The chalice is another symbol of the Goddess, and it is used to hold wine during rituals and to administer magical potions. When it is not in magical use, it is usually filled with water to symbolise the cup of life and the abundance of the universe. The chalice represents the element of Water and it is placed in the western quarter of the altar (the direction of water). It is also associated with the legendary Holy Grail of Arthurian lore. In magic and witchcraft, the chalice stands for the nurturing qualities of the womb.

There are so many beautiful chalices available that it can be quite difficult to make your final choice. Don't rush into buying the first one you come across. Take your time to discover the one that is just perfect for you, as you will be using it for a great many rituals. If a custom-made magical chalice is beyond your budget right now, any stemmed wine glass or pottery goblet will do as a substitute.

Cauldron

Yes, witches do have cauldrons! The cauldron, like the chalice, represents the womb and the element of Water, but due to its transformative powers it is also linked to the fifth element of Akasha, or spirit. As the cauldron was once used for cooking, transforming raw ingredients into nutritious meals, in magic its function is to transform anything in our lives that we are not altogether happy with. Spell papers and candles are often burnt within the safety of a cast-iron cauldron, where they transform our magical wishes and dreams into reality, and magical potions to transform sickness into health are stirred there. The cauldron can also be filled with water and used as a scrying tool, enabling the witch to see a glimpse of the possible future or find a solution to a particular problem.

The cauldron is closely associated with the Crone aspect of the Triple Goddess, and as such it is the sacred tool of the Dark Mother. Therefore it can be used to attune with goddesses of this aspect, such as Cerridwen, Hecate, Circe and the Morrigan. Custom-made magical cauldrons are available in all sizes from most occult stores, but if you cannot find one to suit your budget, you can use a dark-coloured, heatproof casserole dish instead. The cauldron is, after all, simply a large cooking pot!

Besom

This is the traditional name for a witch's broom. Besoms are used within the Craft to sweep away negative energies prior to working magic. They are also used in fertility rites, as the broom is symbolic of the union of male and female in that the stave penetrates the brush. In the Wiccan wedding ceremony, known as a handfasting, the newly pledged couple jump over the broom together as a sign that they are entering into a new phase of life. Thus the besom also has associations with portals and magical doorways, and it is for this reason that one is placed across the entrance to any room a witch wishes to protect. In some traditions brooms are also an invitation to the nature spirits, or faery folk, to take up residence within the home.

Divination tools

Divination tools come in many guises, and most witches have at least one or two in their box of tricks! The most popular are probably decks of cards such as the Tarot, the Celtic tree oracle, faerie and angel oracles, animal oracles and so on. Rune stones are very popular too, as are ogham sticks and the Eastern I Ching. Of course, the most famous fortune-telling device is the crystal ball, and many

witches do use this tool in their divinations. Other types of divination tool include dark-glass scrying mirrors, pendulums and spirit boards.

If you like the idea of divination and fortune-telling, use whichever tool you feel most drawn towards. Try to concentrate on learning to use it properly before moving on to a different tool. Divination takes a lot of practice and you will need to be patient with yourself. It may also help to set aside a regular time each day to practise with your chosen method of divination. In this way you will find that your mind becomes more open to the tool you are using, and in turn your focus and overall performance will become much stronger.

Consumable tools

In addition to all the ritual and divination tools described above, witches also use a variety of other tools to make their magic happen. Most of these tools are consumable and so will need to be replaced regularly, as they form the vital ingredients of spells and rituals. Items such as candles, oils, incenses, dried herbs, Bach flower remedies, tea-lights and crystals will need to be kept in stock, though you needn't buy them all at once.

Most witches keep a few basic oils and so on in store and then add to their main supply when a spell calls for particular items. Witches also generally keep a selection of coloured ribbons, cottons, pens, paper and balloons handy too, so that we can whip up a spell and make magic whenever the need arises. In this way we are always prepared and can cast a spell whenever we want to.

Altars

An altar created specifically for the purposes of witchcraft and spell-casting is a place of great power. Most witches have some kind of altar within their home; however, the need to create altars is almost innate in us. Even those people who don't follow any form of spiritual path tend to have collections of photos, treasures and nic-nacs gathered together and arranged with care. This is known as a subliminal altar, meaning that it has been created in an unconscious way. Witches' altars, however, are consciously created and dedicated to magic and witchcraft.

The altar helps you to connect with your feminine power and woman's wisdom, so it is vital to your craft that you have some kind of special magical space for your rituals and spells to take place in. In some cases the altar is permanently set up, so that it is always available and ready for use and can serve as a daily reminder of your chosen path and an affirmation of your power. A permanent altar will fill your home with magical energies and very positive vibrations. My own altar is a permanent one, but this kind of arrangement doesn't suit everybody. Some witches choose to put all their tools away after working magic and set up their altar only for the duration of the spell. This may be necessary if there are small children in the house or if a partner or other family members are not magical practitioners themselves. Choose whichever method best suits you, your circumstances and your lifestyle.

The advantage of an occasional altar is that you can set it up wherever you need to make magic. With a permanent altar, you need to choose your location carefully. It should be placed in a quiet and private area of the house. A bedroom can be ideal, or you may prefer a study or spare room. Make sure your chosen altar surface is both sturdy and large enough to hold all your magical tools and still provide enough work space for spell-casting. A chest of drawers, a table or a chest are all ideal altar surfaces. Alternatively, you can invest in a custom-made altar from an occult store. These are useful, as they often incorporate cupboards, drawers, secret compartments and built-in candle-holders, magic mirrors, pentacles and so on. They are excellent for storing your tools and offer ample work space, but they can be expensive.

Once you have chosen your altar and decided upon its location, clean it thoroughly. If you wish, you can then drape a pretty cloth over it. Place two white candles in tall candlesticks towards the back of the altar. These are called illuminator candles and should be lit each time you chant a charm or blessing, or perform a spell. Next place your pentacle between these candles and put any representations of the Goddess and God you may have in front of the candlesticks. Place your wand on the right side of the altar, towards the East; your chalice on the left, in the West; and your athame directly in front of you, in the South. Finally, add a small container of sea salt to purify the space and fill your chalice with fresh water to ensure that your cup of life is always full.

Always keep your altar clean and well cared for. Add fresh flowers, crystals, incense and oil-burners if you wish, and make your altar personal to you. Spend a little time here each day, attuning with the magical energies of the universe and getting in touch with your own personal power and feminine magic.

The Book of Shadows

The Book of Shadows, sometimes humorously referred to as the BOS, is a witch's journal of magic. Some witches treat their Book of Shadows like a diary and write down everything they did in a particular ritual or spell. Other witches simply collect together a series of their most powerful spells and rituals and put them in one volume. My own Book of Shadows has poems, Craft lore and family history incorporated into it, as well as spells and rituals that I have written at various points in my life. The spells chosen for my Book of Shadows are those that have proved to be very effective. I also add pictures, dried flowers and photographs to give my Book a very personal feel.

Traditionally, a Book of Shadows should be handwritten by the witch and viewed by no-one else. It is added to over time and becomes a testament of the witch's life within the Craft. It is usually buried or burnt with the witch in the event of her death, or it may be passed down to the next generation if witchcraft is part of the family heritage. Some famous witches have chosen to bequeath their Books of Shadows to the Witchcraft Museum in The Harbour, Boscastle, Cornwall, England rather then have them destroyed upon their death.

To begin your own Book of Shadows you will need to obtain a large hardbound notebook. In the front write your magical name, if you choose to use one, or your given name. Then copy into it any witchy poems you like or spells you have written. Add Goddess and God invocations, chants and charms, spells and rituals, and so on. Creating a Book of Shadows is an ongoing project, but once you begin you will find that you are creating your very own version of the

Craft. As a very important tool, the Book of Shadows is usually protected by magic, generally in the form of a protection spell such as the one below.

To protect your book of shadows

You will need a length of black or red ribbon and two protective silver charms for this spell. These are available from most New Age and occult stores. Good charms to choose are pentagrams, pentacles, crescent moons and triquetras. Alternatively, pick two little silver witch charms, gemstone pendants or even small lockets.

◆ Place the charms on your pentacle to charge for three days and nights.

◆ Pass the length of ribbon up the spine of your Book, making sure that it is long enough for both ends to hang below the book covers. This will act as your page marker.

◆ Once the charms are fully charged, sew the first charm onto one end of the ribbon, as you do so saying:

> As I stitch and as I sew,
> I raise the power as I go.
> The magic of each little charm
> Keeps my Shadows safe from harm.
> From those who pry and those who peek,
> From prying eyes this Book they keep.
> As I will it shall be so!
> I snip the thread and let the power go!

◆ Sew the second charm onto the other end of the ribbon, as you do so, repeating the rhyme.

To cast a magic circle

The magic circle is an invisible boundary that keeps all negative energies away from you and your spell-casting. It should be cast before any spell work or divination you perform. This is how to do it.

◆ Stand with your arm outstretched and, pointing with your finger, wand or athame, walk around (or turn if the space is small) in a circle three times in a clockwise direction. (The Wiccan term for clockwise is 'deosil'). As you do so, imagine a stream of blue light forming a circle around you and your altar.

◆ Now imagine that this light expands upwards and below you, forming a sphere of blue light.

◆ Clap once and say:

This circle is sealed!

After you have worked your magic, the circle must be taken down again so that the spell is released. Do this by moving or turning in an anticlockwise (or widdershins) direction three times and imagine the blue light being drawn back into your finger, wand or athame.

Practise casting and taking down your magic circle on a regular basis until you get accustomed to the subtle shift in energies that takes place. Remember to cast a circle before every spell, divination and ritual you perform, and to take it down again afterwards.

Witchcraft is ...

For those who feel the seasons
Flowing through their veins,
For those who watch the snow fall
And dance in spring-time rains,
For those who see the autumn leaf
As the most precious gold on Earth,
For those who see a foal born
And wonder at the miracle of birth,
For those who touch the moon beams
And have starlight in their eyes,
For those who watch the clouds drift
On their journey across the skies,
For those who love the mountains
And take in their awesome might,
For those who watch the eagle
And gasp at his graceful flight,
For those who feel the volcano
And marvel at nature's power,
For those who smile at a rainbow
Invoked by a summer shower,
For those who love the ocean,
Who love the crashing of the waves,
For those who want the freedom
Our Earth-bound spirit craves,
For those who walk the sandy shore
Understanding the sea-gulls' cries,
For those who walk a hidden path,
A witch of the Craft of the Wise.

Morgana

The Wheel of the Year

The witches' sabbats are a series of festivals that celebrate the turning of the seasons. There are eight sabbats in all, approximately six weeks apart, and they can be divided into two groups, the greater sabbats and the lesser sabbats. The four greater sabbats are Imbolc, Beltane, Lughnasadh and Samhain, while the four lesser sabbats are Yule, Ostara, Litha and Mabon. These last four sabbats mark the equinoxes and the solstices, so their actual dates vary slightly from year to year, though they generally fall between the 19th and 22nd of the month.

The eight sabbats are known collectively as the Wheel of the Year. They are a time when special rituals and magical workings are performed to acknowledge the changing season and to draw upon the power of this special time. The eight sabbats are a way for us to touch base with the natural world and see what is going on around us. They also help us to accept the cyclical nature of the universe and the endless pattern of birth, death and rebirth.

Of course, the sabbats, like many other aspects of the Craft, have changed and evolved over time. But at their core their message remains the same, and modern witches celebrate the same seasonal cycle that our ancestors did. This means that when we celebrate the sabbats we are also connecting with our heritage as witches.

Below is a brief description of each sabbat, along with a simple ritual for you to perform for each of the festivals. Learning to honour and respect the natural world around us is a vital part of being a witch, and celebrating the sabbats is a great way to begin. If you would like to learn more about seasonal magic and spell-casting, see my book *The Witch's Almanac*.

Samhain – 31 October

Why do we begin with Samhain? Because it is the witches' New Year and the first point on the magical cycle. Samhain is more popularly known by its Christian name, Halloween. In the past this was the last day of the old Celtic calendar. As such it is a time for letting go of anything that no longer serves us. Of course, everyone knows that this is the night of the witches, and Samhain is one of our most important festivals. It's also a great time for getting out all your witchy clothes and regalia and knowing that you'll still blend right in! Many witchy events are going on at this time of year, so it could be the perfect opportunity for you to meet people of a like mind and with similar interests.

Samhain means 'summer's end', and it is at this time of year that the darkness really begins to take over. The nights are long and cold and the general atmosphere is quite eerie. Magically speaking, it is at this time of year that the mystical veil between our world and the Otherworld is at its thinnest, enabling spirits and ghosts to pass freely across for a short time. Samhain is traditionally a time for honouring the dead in general and in particular loved ones who have passed on. This accounts for the spookiness people notice during the dark season. It also goes some way towards explaining why more elderly people pass on during the darker half of the year: their crossing is made easier by the thinning of the spiritual veil.

The children's game of Trick or Treat has its foundations in the old Roman festival of Saturnalia (which took place in January), at which a Lord of Misrule was chosen and allowed to run riot! Echoes of this tradition could still be found in the Middle Ages, when every castle had its fool or jester.

Samhain is a great time for a gathering, so you could celebrate by attending an open sabbat festival, going to a bonfire or some sort of 'fright night', or having your own Halloween party with a group of friends. Storytelling is a traditional part of the dark season too, so telling or reading ghost stories would be particularly appropriate, as would ghost walks or a visit to a reputedly haunted house. Samhain is a time for spooky fun, and since it is right in the middle of the zodiac sign of Scorpio, you could find yourself feeling extra sexy too!

Despite its frivolous side, this festival is a powerful time with an important magical significance, and most witches indulge in some kind of magical activity on this night, divination and scrying being a traditional part of this sabbat.

Decorating the altar for Samhain

As the Wheel of the Year turns, you should set up an altar that is in tune with the sabbat. For Samhain witches use black and orange, so a black altar cloth and orange candles could form the basis of your altar set-up. To this you could add a stereotypical witch figure,

complete with black cat, broomstick and cauldron. This would represent the Crone or Dark Mother, as this is her associated sabbat. A hollowed-out pumpkin lantern is especially fitting, and your cauldron should take centre stage, as you will be using it for the ritual below. Include any other Halloween or magical decorations you like, plus photographs of any dead loved ones you wish to honour and remember. Finally, add a plate of gingerbread cookies, perhaps in the shape of ghosts or pumpkins, and fill your chalice with cider or juice.

Samhain ritual

Samhain is the time when we let go of anything that no longer serves us and release anything that may be holding us back.

◆ Light your orange altar candles and place a tea-light in your pumpkin lantern.

◆ Sit for a few moments thinking of all that you need to release from your life. This may be painful, particularly if you are letting go of a lost loved one or a shattered dream. If tears come, just let them flow – it is all part of the release.

◆ Once you have decided what you need to let go of, write each thing down on a separate slip of paper. Then speak the following ritual charm:

*Dark Mother, powerful Crone, I call you here this magical
night and ask that you take away these aspects of my life that
no longer serve me. I give them to you freely and ask you to
take them with you into the Shadow World that my life may
be transformed. I honour the dark season of nature and accept
that all must die in order to be reborn. Blessed be!*

◆ Now light the slips of paper one by one from the altar candles and allow each one to burn in your cauldron of transformation. As you do so say:

I release —— from my life.

◆ Once all your slips have been burnt, sit a while at the altar, enjoying a ritual feast of cakes and ale (or ginger biscuits and juice) and concentrating on the sabbat and feeling its energies.

◆ When you are ready, blow out the altar candles and go and have fun with the rest of your planned Samhain activities.

Yule – on or around 21 December

Yule is the festival of the winter solstice. On this night we enjoy more than 12 hours of darkness. After this, the longest night of the year, the days will begin to grow gradually longer and the nights will shorten. For this reason pagans view Yule as the rebirth of the sun, which will grow stronger and stronger in the months to come. With the return of the sun, the Earth will awaken from its barren winter sleep and life will be renewed.

Holding some kind of feast and festival in mid-winter to brighten up the long, dark, cold nights and to give people something to look forward to is an ancient tradition that has passed into many of the newer religions. We saw in Chapter 1 how the early Christians overlaid paganism with Christian meaning (see page 14). This is also evident in the pagan festivals, in particular Ostara (the Christian Easter) and Yule (the Christian Christmas). Father Christmas, riding through the sky on a magical sleigh, has links with the Horned God of the Wild Hunt. The bestowal of blessings in the form of gifts and the title Father both echo the Witches' God, and the antlered reindeer pulling the sleigh is sacred to him.

The tradition of bringing holly and ivy into the house as a form of decoration also has pagan associations. The holly represents the pagan God, while the ivy is associated with the Goddess. These sacred plants have long been used by witches for their magical powers of protection, defence, binding and fertility.

Another pagan Yuletide tradition that we still enjoy today is that of the Yule log. This is a classic example of how spiritual traditions change and evolve but simply refuse to go away! In the past, the Yule log was a huge trunk of firewood, preferably of oak, ash or pine, that was lit on solstice night and left to burn throughout the sabbat. A piece of the wood was always saved and used to light the Yule log the following year, keeping up a magical link from one year to the next.

Of course, the only Yule log most of us enjoy these days is a calorie-filled confection of chocolate, sponge and cream! But there is no reason why you cannot eat it with reverence, bearing in mind the cake's historical origins. I usually place three birthday candles in the log and let them burn for a while before cutting the log itself. The three candles represent past, present and future and also the three aspects of the Goddess, maiden, mother and crone. Putting the candles on the yule log also reminds me of the symbolism of the Yule log and the fact that Yule is a fire festival, celebrating the return of the sun.

The Yuletide tree is a reminder that life is ever present, even in the depths of winter. Although this tradition didn't take off in the UK until the reign of Queen Victoria, it is now a cornerstone of both Yuletide and Christmas festivities.

Mistletoe, however, has a much older origin. It is thought that this little plant was first used by the ancient Greeks and was later adopted by the Celts and the druids. Mistletoe is a sacred plant within pagan, and especially druidic, lore because it symbolises the seed of the pagan God. As a protective plant, it is said to guard against thunder, lightning and evil spirits, and it is also strongly associated with fertility, love and luck in relationships – hence to kiss beneath the mistletoe is to bless the relationship or invoke a new love.

Decorating the altar for Yule

The main colours for this sabbat are red and green, and you might like to add a touch of gold to represent the return of the sun. Choose candles and an altar cloth in these colours and add any Yuletide symbols you like; sun-shaped ornaments are appropriate, as is a figure of Herne the Hunter, Father Christmas, stags, reindeer or the Snow Queen. Representations of snow flakes, icicles, and silver stars can be added too. Make sure you have an uncut chocolate Yule log with three birthday candles on it ready for lighting, and fill your chalice with mulled wine.

Yule ritual

♦ As dusk falls on the night of the winter solstice, go to your altar, taking with you a large pillar candle in a deep-red or -green hue. If this is scented with a seasonal fragrance, so much the better.

♦ Light the altar candles and sit for a moment thinking of all that the sabbat has to offer and all that it represents. Think of how this festival has changed through history and yet has survived the take-over attempt by the early Christians and is still perhaps the most significant holiday in the modern calendar.

♦ Once you have attuned with the sabbat, place your scented Yuletide candle on a platter and light it. This represents the flame of the fire festival, and you should allow it to burn throughout your sabbat celebrations. Next, light the three birthday candles on the Yule log and say the following charm:

As darkness fails and light returns,
All that seemed dead shall grow.
As the sun bursts forth on a frosty morn,
The Earth is bathed in a fiery glow.
Welcome Sun God! Bring your light!
Welcome Sun God! I honour you this night!

♦ Blow out the candles on the Yule log and make a wish for your future. Then, using your athame, make the first cut in the chocolate log and enjoy a slice along with your mulled wine.

♦ Enjoy the rest of the sabbat and celebrate in your own way.

Imbolc – 2 February

Imbolc celebrates the first stirrings of new life that are taking place deep in the womb of the Earth. On the surface, the world may still be a barren place, but we know that spring is just around the corner and that the Earth is beginning to wake from its long winter sleep. Imbolc is a festival of light, when we recognise the growing strength of the sun and the subtle lengthening of the days. It is the time of the Maiden Goddess, and this sabbat is sacred to Bride (pronounced *Breed*), the Celtic goddess of poetry, writing, art, smithcraft and music. Bride is also a goddess associated with the hearth and home, and is said to protect women during childbirth. In addition, she is said to bring inspiration to writers, poets, painters and so on, and is a patron of all the creative arts.

An old tradition for this sabbat is that of Bride's bed. This is a small box or basket with pretty fabric laid within to form a bed. A corn dolly representing Bride is laid in the bed and the whole thing is placed on the hearth for the duration of the Imbolc festival. This is said to attract Bride's blessings to your home and will bring luck and happiness throughout the year. Another tradition is to light candles throughout the whole home to represent the growing daylight. These days, less romantically, most witches turn on all the lights in the house to satisfy this custom, as it is never a good idea to leave lots of candles burning unattended! Try to make sure you have several candles burning in the room in which you are celebrating the sabbat though.

Decorating the altar for Imbolc

Imbolc is all about purity and light, so the colours of this sabbat are white and silver. Your altar should be draped with a white cloth and decorated with white flowers – virginal snowdrops and lilies are particularly appropriate. White and silver candles should be used in abundance. Fill your chalice with milk or white wine and place croissants on a platter to represent the crescent moon and the Maiden aspect of the Goddess.

Imbolc ritual

◆ After dressing the altar and putting Bride's bed in place, light all your ritual candles and an incense of your choice.

◆ Sit for a few moments contemplating the changing of the season and acknowledging the quickening that is taking place in the Earth, which will soon burst forth into spring.

◆ When you are ready, say the following ritual charm:

Here is Imbolc, feast of flames;
Winter ends as sunlight gains.
Goddess Bride, I call you here;
Bring the Sun God, strong and clear.
Goddess of so many names,
We welcome you as winter wanes.
Lay your blessings beside Bride's bed;
It is the Old Ways we now tread.
Power now to us reveal

With the turning of the Wheel.

◆ Perform any magical spells or divinations you have planned, then drink your wine and enjoy your crescent cakes. Continue to celebrate the sabbat in your own way.

Ostara – on or around 21 March

Ostara is the sabbat of the spring equinox. This is one of the two times of year when the world is in perfect balance and the hours of light and dark are exactly equal. From now on the light will increase and the days will grow longer. It is at Ostara that spring becomes apparent – birds sing and build their nests, daffodils blow in the breeze, the trees flaunt their first budding leaves, and the world is generally waking up as new life takes hold.

Ostara is associated with the Anglo-Saxon spring goddess Eostra, and it is easy to see the link between this pagan goddess of new life and the Christian festival of Easter, which celebrates Christ's return to life. Eostra's sacred animals are the rabbit and the hare, which is where the idea of the Easter bunny comes from. As Eostra is a goddess of fertility, eggs are used to represent her gifts and blessings. (Interestingly Eostra's name is also believed to be the root for the word 'oestrogen', the female hormone that stimulates egg release.) Eggs are a huge part of this sabbat, be they hand-painted decorative ones or the chocolate variety. Your sabbat feast should certainly include the latter! This sabbat is all about fertility and growth, and witches work magic at this time to draw in their life's goals and to fertilise their ideas.

Decorating the altar for Ostara

This is a spring altar, so it should bear a profusion of spring flowers. The colours associated with Ostara are pale-green and lemon-yellow, with a touch of pastel-pink and lilac, so decorate your altar with a cloth and candles of these pretty springtime hues. Every Ostara altar should include some representation of fertility. This could be a little bowl of seeds, a collection of hand-painted eggs, a large chocolate egg or images of new chicks and lambs. A figure or picture of a rabbit or hare should also be included to represent the goddess Eostra. Fill your chalice with fresh spring water and add a platter of rabbit-shaped cookies to enjoy after the ritual.

Ostara ritual

For this spring ritual you will need a hard-boiled egg; a marker pen; and paints, nail polish and so on with which to decorate the egg.

◆ Go to your spring altar and light the candles and an incense of your choice.

◆ Spend a few moments centring yourself and concentrating on all that the sabbat of Ostara symbolises and that spring has to offer. Feel the joy of rebirth and new life in your heart.

◆ Now think of something you want to bring into your life – your own personal goal. This could be a new job, general abundance, the conception and birth of a healthy child, the success of a creative venture or a new business opportunity, or whatever is relevant to you.

- Once you know what your goal is, write it on the shell of the hard-boiled egg using the marker pen. Now use the paints and varnishes to decorate the egg. This is now a symbol of your goal and a representation of the fertility of your dream.
- Place the egg in an egg cup and stand it at the centre of your altar for the duration of the sabbat. Then enjoy your feast and continue to celebrate in your own way.
- The next day, take your spell egg outside and bury it in the earth, as you do so saying:

Goddess Eostra, take this your symbol and fertilise my dreams.
So mote it be!

Beltane – 30 April

Beltane is the main fertility festival of the witches' calendar. It is at this time that we celebrate the growth of nature, the miracle of pregnancy and birth, the loving union of man and woman, and the great power of sexuality. As spring moves towards summer, many people find that they feel more sexual. This can put an added spark into a long-term relationship, or if you are single it can make you more open to the idea of a new relationship. Beltane works its magic on everyone; no-one is immune to the vast fertile power that now holds the earth in its grip! Witches make use of this power by drawing it into their spell-castings as they work towards the growth and fulfilment of their goals, dreams and ambitions.

In pagan terms, Beltane marks the beginning of summer and is named after the sun god Bel. It is a fire festival, and bonfires were once lit on hilltops to honour this god. These were known as balefires and were beacons to welcome the warmth and heat of summer.

The most famous Beltane tradition is, of course, the May Pole. The pole itself is a phallic representation of masculinity, and the wreath of flowers placed around the top of the pole represents the feminine. The dance around the May Pole is symbolic of the union of male and female. As it proceeds, the ribbons wrap around the pole, allowing the wreath of flowers to descend the length of the pole in a figurative version of the sexual act. Although superficially it doesn't appear to be the sexiest dance in the world, it was still considered raunchy enough to be banned by the Puritans. Fortunately, King Charles II revived the tradition of May Pole dancing, and it can still be seen today as part of Beltane and May Day celebrations everywhere.

Beltane is also a great time to go for a woodland walk. In days gone by, people would go out at dusk on Beltane and stay out all night. They would return with the dawn, bringing with them branches of hawthorn blossom, or May blossom as it was also known, and the fresh flowers of the fields and woodlands. This custom is where the term 'go a-maying' originated, and it is still practised in some rural areas of the UK.

Decorating the altar for Beltane

The colours of Beltane are red and white, so you should use an altar cloth and candles in these colours. Add red and white ribbons too, to symbolise the ribbons of the May Pole. Vases filled with May blossom, lilacs or bluebells would be appropriate, as would a wreath of flowers or a few tendrils of ivy. A figure or picture of the god Pan is especially in keeping with the untamed energies of this sabbat, but remember what we said earlier about working with Pan (see page 54) and expect a few surprises! Fill your chalice with red wine or red grape juice and add a platter of heart-shaped cookies for your ritual feast afterwards.

Beltane ritual

◆ Go to your altar and light the candles, together with a lovely summer-scented incense.

◆ Sit for a while and think of all the wonderful things Beltane has to offer, then say the following sabbat charm in honour of the season:

> *Here is Beltane, feast of lovers;*
> *Earth grows warm where sunlight covers.*
> *Joy and laughter shall abound*
> *As we dance the sacred May Pole round.*
> *We gather blooms and go a-maying*
> *Till break of dawn brings the day in.*
> *We welcome summer with the morn*
> *And conjure love by oak, ash and thorn!*

◆ Enjoy your Beltane feast and celebrate the sabbat in whatever way suits you.

Litha – on or around 21 June

Litha is the sabbat of the summer solstice, the longest day of the year. Midsummer's day is the peak of the summer time, when the sun is at its strongest and has reached its highest point in the sky. From now on the days will gradually shorten and the dark season will return. The sun will become steadily weaker, and if you watch closely you will notice the difference as the light begins to change and we move into July and August.

This is the time of the Mother aspect of the Goddess, when the world is fruitful, giving and abundant. It is a most productive time of year, when we enjoy all that summer has to offer. However, in Wiccan mythology, this is also the time when the Sun God dies and becomes instead Lord of the Otherworld, bringing us the darker half of the year. This serves as a reminder that we should make the most of the summer days, as autumn will soon be upon us. It is also traditional to make some kind of pilgrimage on the summer solstice, hence the popularity of such places as Avebury, Stonehenge and Glastonbury at this time of year – although you may prefer to visit a more local beauty spot, and this is fine too.

Decorating the altar for Litha

The colours of this sabbat are the colours of the sun – gold, yellow and burnished orange – so use altar cloths and candles accordingly. Add any sun-shaped ornaments and tea-light-holders you may have and a vase of bright-yellow flowers. You could also add a single holly leaf to represent the God's transformation from Sun God to Dark Lord. Fill your chalice with orange juice, eat oranges and add a platter of ginger biscuits or orange slices to represent the sun for your feast.

Litha ritual

◆ The best ritual for this sabbat is to get out and about for the greatest part of the day, enjoying the summer sunshine.

◆ When you return, go to your altar and light the candles to represent the sun. Think of all that you enjoy throughout the summer months.

◆ When you are ready, snuff out the candles – to represent the death of the sun – and say:

Go freely with our love, Sun God. We embrace your transformation and will welcome your return as the Dark Lord. Blessed be!

◆ Take your ritual feast outside and watch the sun set and the Sun God go down into the Otherworld. The longest day is over.

Lughnasadh – 1 August

Lughnasadh is a harvest festival celebrating the gifts of corn and grain and the generous sacrifice of John Barleycorn. It is named after the old Celtic god Lugh. It is traditional to bake bread on this day in honour of the harvest and the corn spirit. Lughnasadh is a time for giving thanks for all we enjoy and all that the year has brought to us so far.

Decorating the altar for Lughnasadh

Choose the colours of the harvest for this sabbat – gold, yellow, green and bronze – and use them for your candles and altar cloth. Add some kind of corn dolly to your altar and fill your chalice with ale or shandy. Place a platter of bread rolls ready for the feast.

Lughnasadh ritual

You will need to perform this ritual outside, taking with you your chalice of ale and the platter of bread rolls, together with a stick of your favourite incense and a lighter or matches.

◆ Find a pretty, natural spot in your garden and think of three things that you are grateful for in your life right now.

◆ Take up your chalice and say:
   I give thanks for (name the first thing you are grateful for).

◆ Now pour the ale onto the ground, as you do so saying:
   I give to the Goddess that the Goddess may give to me.

◆ Take up the bread and say
   I give thanks for (name the second thing you are grateful for).

◆ Break the bread into pieces and scatter it on the ground, as you do so saying:
   I give to the earth that the earth may give to me.

◆ Light the stick of incense and say:
   I give thanks for (name the third thing you are grateful for).

◆ Stake the incense into the ground, as you do so saying:
   I give to the universe that the universe may give to me.

◆ Bow your head and say:
   Blessed be!

◆ Now repeat the following ritual charm:
   As summer fades to autumn's gold,
   We begin to see our dreams unfold.
   For the free will of all and with harm to none,
   I say farewell to the God of Sun.
   Spirit to spirit and heart to heart,
   Merry we meet and merry we part.
   In honour of the Goddess and God,
   Blessed be!

◆ Go back inside and enjoy a harvest-inspired ritual feast as you allow your altar candles to burn for a while.

Mabon

Mabon is the sabbat of the autumn equinox. Once again the world hangs in balance and the hours of light and dark are equal, though this time the days will become shorter and darkness will prevail. It is autumn. The first leaves are falling and the autumn mist is swirling. There is the tang of fresh fallen leaves in the air, and we know that summer is now over and the nights are drawing in.

This sabbat is about welcoming and preparing for the dark season and planning ahead for the winter. The veil between our world and the Otherworld is thinning, and the spookiness begins to creep up on us out of the autumn fog. Most witches use this time to prepare their homes for the winter, laying down rugs, putting up thicker curtains, and doing any last-minute repairs to the home, car and garden. We also stock up cupboards, freezers and our magical cabinets so that we begin the dark season with a feeling of abundance and plenty.

Decorating the altar for Mabon

Choose autumn colours for your altar cloth and candles, and use acorns, pine cones and fallen leaves to decorate the altar. Fill your chalice with blackberry or apple juice and put a berry pie on your ritual platter with a jug of cream for the feast.

Wabon ritual

◆ Light your altar candles and sit and think about the dark season that is to come. Feel the shift in energies around you and the spookiness that will increase as the darkness strengthens its grip on the world.

◆ When you feel ready, welcome the Dark Lord of the Otherworld with the following ritual charm:

Welcome, Dark Lord, master of night.
Welcome, Dark Lord, as summer takes flight.
Bring your gifts of wisdom and strength,
As nights so black increase in length;
Bring the rains, the frosts and mists.
I honour and welcome the dark season's gifts.
Blessed be!

◆ Enjoy your feast and continue to celebrate the sabbat in your own way.

The Wheel of the Year is an intrinsic part of the Craft and, as you can see, all the sabbats relate in some way to the seasonal path of the sun. But there is another power that witches call upon too – that of the beautiful enchanting moon in her realm of night ...

Awaiting the Mother Phase

Watching the moon grow round and full,
Wishing my womb would swell and fill,
Seeing the Mother phase high in the sky,
Hearing the clock as time passes by,
Counting the days, hoping to be late,
Feeling trapped in a barren state,
Longing to blossom, flower and bloom,
Yearning to nurture the seed in my womb.
Yet every month the crimson flow streams,
Washing away my motherhood dreams.
And then the cycle begins once more,
As we try to create Life deep in my core,
Hoping and praying, letting it be ...
But when will the Mother phase welcome me?

Morgana

The Silver Wheel of the Moon

With its inky-black sky, shimmering stars and glowing moon, most witches find the realm of night intoxicating. There is something truly magical about the dark hours; it seems as if anything can happen when shadowy clouds drift across the face of the silver moon. On a warm summer's night when the stars are shining brightly, the world seems almost like fairyland, and a sense of mystery and magic fills the atmosphere. The night is quiet yet active, dark yet filled with light, peaceful yet slightly unnerving. And to the practising witch, the night is full of magical power just waiting to be used.

Midnight is of course the witching hour, and lots of witches choose to perform their magic during the night. This can add to the magical atmosphere and may help the witch to get into the right frame of mind for spell-casting. There is a more practical reason for this too, in that at night there is little chance of distraction from ringing telephones, the noise of televisions and stereos, or visitors at the door. If you have children, they are tucked up in bed asleep and unlikely to interrupt you. Working magic in the middle of the night virtually guarantees that you can give your spell work your complete and undivided attention, and, as we have seen, this is essential if your spell is to be effective. Of course, working magic during the day is perfectly acceptable, especially if you are calling upon the powers of the sun. However, at night it is easier to switch off from distractions and tune out anything that isn't part of your spell. In the beginning, you will probably find it easier to work your magic during the night.

And, of course, the night has one source of power that is an intrinsic part of all spell-casting – the moon.

The mystery of the moon

The moon holds an incredible power over the Earth. Its magnetic force governs the pattern of the tides and has a strong influence over the menstrual cycle of women. It is a familiar sight to all of us. Men have walked upon its surface, yet still the moon retains an air of mystery. Like the Mona Lisa, the moon smiles down upon us, and we can only guess what her secret may be as she waxes and wanes according to her cosmic pattern.

For centuries, writers and poets have tried to describe the magic and mystery of the moon, referring to her as queen of the night, queen of heaven, queen of stars, silver wheel, silver orb and much more. Yet still the perfect definition eludes us. In my mind the moon is a beautiful glamorous mystery, whose immense power enchants all of us on some level.

The lunar cycle

The phases of the moon are an important part of spell-casting, and you will need to be able to recognise which phase the moon is in in order to time your spells correctly. Interestingly, the phases of the moon are the same all over the globe, so that when it's full moon here in the UK, it's full moon on the other side of the world too.

The correct term for a single lunar cycle – from new moon to new moon – is a lunation. It takes approximately 29 days for the moon to move through one lunation, and so already we can see the link between the lunar cycle and the female menstrual cycle, which takes approximately 28 days. This is perhaps the main reason why witches view the moon as feminine and a natural link with the energies of the Great Goddess. We will be looking at this in more detail later (see page 128), but for now let's consider the lunar cycle, its significance in witchcraft and how you can draw upon its powers for various types of spell.

New moon

The new moon appears as a thin sliver of light in the sky. It is sometimes called a bride's moon. This is a time of rebirth and new beginnings, so all spells for new ventures, new projects and new beginnings should be cast during this phase. The new moon is also good for spells concerning innocence and childhood and for general cleansings. In witchcraft, the new moon is associated with the maiden aspect of the Triple Goddess.

Waxing moon

This is the time when the moon is growing, expanding from new to full. The waxing moon appears as a crescent in the sky, its points facing left. Its light gradually increases, appearing to spread from right to left. This phase should be used for all spells that work to bring something into your life, and it is particularly good for spells of growth and fertility. This phase, too, is associated with the Maiden aspect of the Triple Goddess.

Full moon

This phase, when the moon appears as a perfect circle in the sky, is the most powerful, and all spells can be cast effectively during it. In witchcraft this phase of the moon is known as the silver wheel and is associated with the Mother aspect of the Triple Goddess. You should also be aware that the night before and the night after the full moon are considered to be just as powerful in magical terms, effectively giving three whole nights of full moon power.

Waning moon

This is the time when the moon grows smaller in the sky, appearing as a crescent again, but this time with its points facing right, so that it makes a C shape. Witches use this phase to cast spells to remove unhelpful influences from their lives. These influences may range from poverty to bad habits, bad relationships and negative people. So if you want to rid your life gently of something, use this phase. The waning moon is associated with the Crone aspect of the Triple Goddess.

Dark moon

The moon is said to be dark when it isn't visible in the sky. This is usually during the three nights prior to the new moon. This is traditionally a time of rest, and the only magic worked during this phase is banishing spells (which push something away from you) and binding spells (which freeze something's influence over you). This phase, too, is associated with the Crone.

Blue moon

A blue moon occurs when there is more than one full moon within a single calendar month, the second being the blue moon. This only happens once every few years, hence the expression 'once in a blue moon'. It is a most magical time, particularly if it is immediately followed or preceded by a sabbat. Blue moon energy is rare and should never be wasted. This is a time for setting long-term goals and for casting spells to help manifest your dreams. Make sure you use this moon's magic wisely.

As you can see, each phase of the moon is linked to a particular kind of magic, and this is the first thing to take into consideration when casting and creating your own spells. If in any doubt, work at the time of the full moon, which is good for all aspects of magic.

Moon wisdom

As the most powerful time in the lunar cycle, full moon is the traditional time for coven meetings to take place. Whether a member of a coven or a solitary, every witch performs an esbat – or ritual to celebrate the moon – at each full moon, and you should set aside a little time for your own full moon rites. Moon magic is an incredibly ancient practice and harks back to a time when life was lived by a lunar calendar rather than the solar one we are familiar with today.

As a solitary witch it is important that you get to know the moon. Look for her each night. Notice how she rises in a diagonal line, sometimes becoming visible even before the sun has set. Notice how she moves through the sky in relation to your house. Is there a window that is perfect for moon-gazing on a cold winter's night? Notice how the moon beams bathe the world in a mystical silver light, giving familiar sights a shimmering new look.

If you have pets, you may notice a subtle change in their behaviour as the new or full moon approaches. My own cat, Pyewackett, simply refuses to stay indoors on the night of the full moon, no matter how cold or wet the weather is! You may also notice a change in yourself, particularly at full moon. Maybe you sleep better, or perhaps you have strange dreams that leave you feeling as if you've been on a journey somewhere. Many witches experience prophetic dreams at this time. Maybe you find that you are more clumsy and accident-prone. More accidents happen at the full moon and more births are recorded at this time too. So when strange things happen in everyday life and people laughingly attribute it to the full moon, there is actually some truth in what they are saying. The moon has far more influence over us than most people are aware of.

Creating a lunar altar

A great way to begin drawing down the magical power of the moon is to create a small lunar altar. The colours of the moon are white and silver, so drape your chosen surface in a satin cloth and add silver and white candles. Add some kind of crescent moon ornament and scatter a few confetti stars over the altar cloth.

As the moon governs the tides, it has strong links with the ocean, so sea shells and dried starfish are appropriate, as is a glass or crystal bowl filled with water and floating candles. Add another bowl filled with crystals and gems such as opal, moonstone, clear quartz, snowy quartz, pearls, celestite and the paler varieties of aquamarine. Burn Night Queen incense here on a regular basis, and if you have an affinity with a particular moon goddess, add a picture or statue to represent her. Arianrhod is perfect for a lunar altar (see below).

Arianrhod

Arianrhod, the lady of the silver wheel, after whom this chapter is named, is the Celtic goddess of the moon. She was famed for her beauty and purity and her vast knowledge of the magical arts. It is thought by some that the character of Argante in Arthurian legend is based on her. There are certainly similarities between these two figures, both being magical ladies associated with the realm of the Otherworld. Argante was an elf maid who later became queen of Avalon, while

Arianrhod ruled the heavens and, in some traditions, the Celtic Otherworld.

As a gentle yet powerful moon goddess, Arianrhod is the perfect goddess for neophyte witches to attune with. Her energy is subtle but very magical and extremely feminine. Sit at your lunar altar and say the following invocation to tap into her power (you might like to copy it out using a silver pen and keep it ready on your lunar altar):

> *'Tis Arianrhod's power I feel,*
> *Lady of the Silver Wheel.*
> *Silver moon in sky at night,*
> *Surrounded by stars shining bright,*
> *I draw your light, I feel your power,*
> *Enchanted by the witching hour.*
> *Arianrhod, I call to thee.*
> *Bless my witchcraft! So mote it be!*

Drawing down the moon

Drawing down the moon is the magical term for pulling in the moon's energy and is a standard part of any full moon esbat. It is usually done outdoors, but if you feel more comfortable indoors, perform the ritual at a window where you can see the full moon.

◆ Speak the invocation of Arianrhod above.

◆ Take your athame and, raising both arms above your head, point it towards the moon. Imagine that the athame is absorbing the power and the magic of the moon. You may feel a slight tingle in your fingertips as you do this.

◆ Now say:

> *I am a priestess of the Goddess.*
> *I walk the Old Ways.*
> *I am a weaver of magic and light.*
> *I now draw down the power of the moon.*
> *I take into myself the magic of the Great Goddess.*
> *Blessed be!*

◆ Point the athame towards your heart and imagine that you are drawing the power and light of the moon into yourself.

◆ Continue to honour the full moon by spending a little time at your lunar altar, maybe reading the myths of the moon goddesses. Alternatively, you might prefer to sit in your garden and take in the beauty of a moonlit summer's night.

Moon time

We have seen how the cycle of the moon echoes the menstrual cycle of women. For this reason witches refer to their periods as 'moon time'. When a woman is in her moon time she is at her most powerful. Her senses are heightened, her instincts and intuition are finely tuned, and she is generally more aware of her surroundings and perceptive of others and their emotions. It is also likely that her creativity will come to the fore during moon time, and women who work in the arts may find that they do their best work during their period.

Of course, moon time has its discomforts, such as cramps, headaches, back pain and general irritability, but all these things can be relieved by the simple methods of the wise woman. For example, drinking raspberry tea can help to ease some of the symptoms of PMT, while adding a few drops of geranium oil to your bath water can help to ease aches and pains such as cramps and lower back pain. But perhaps the most effective way to deal with periods and the discomforts they can bring is to change our attitude towards them by accepting menstruation as a sacred part of being a woman and understanding that a woman needs a certain amount of quiet time at this stage in her cycle. In some cultures in the past, women would spend their moon time in a special tent or lodge, where they would relax, take herbal remedies to relieve the discomforts and enjoy the company of other women who were also having their period. It was a time of sisterhood and companionship. They would also work magic and perform divinations, using their moon-time power to its full potential and for the good of the tribe.

Unfortunately, women today don't have the luxury of a moon-time lodge. Instead, we are expected to carry on as normal. This can lead to high levels of stress and the crankiness known as PMT. We've probably all bitten someone's head off for no reason at one time or another during our period. This could simply be our feminine spirit craving a little time out.

For the duration of, and the few days leading up to, their period, most women crave a little more quiet, introspective time. You may struggle to get through an ordinary working day and find that you become more dreamy and absent-minded, lethargic and tired, tearful and over-sensitive. Some women find interacting with people in general, and men in particular, an ordeal during this time. This can be difficult if you're married or living with a partner. However, it is quite natural to want to withdraw from male company at this time. Some women experience problems with technology, particularly computers, as their personal energy field goes through subtle changes. Some, myself included, become clumsy, dropping and breaking things. I personally find that my driving skills regress to the point where I try not to drive for a couple of days.

Finding your goddess cycle

The phase of the moon during her period holds a special significance for the witch, as it determines the direction her increased powers will take and what kind of magic she should be performing at this special time. Most women will fluctuate between the three goddess cycles at various points in their lives. This is quite natural, as the body creates its own patterns. Periods don't always run like clockwork, so while you may be in one goddess cycle now, you may be in a different goddess cycle in six months' time. Keep a close watch on the moon and notice how she relates to your own feminine patterns. The following are the different goddess cycles.

Maiden cycle: new moon to waxing moon

If your period falls on or between the new and waxing moon, you have a Maiden cycle. This means that your moon time powers are best used for spells that bring happiness, laughter and fun. All spells of love and fertility will be doubly powerful if you cast them on the first or second day of your period. The magic you work during your moon time should be with a view to increasing the overall joy in your life. Diana and Artemis are Maiden moon goddesses you might like to attune with during your moon time, so read up on them and work your spells in their name.

Mother cycle: full moon

If the moon is full at the time of your period, you have a Mother cycle. This means that your moon time powers are best directed towards nurturing, healing and abundance magic, so work spells accordingly, keeping in view the bigger picture and your long-term goals as you do so. You may find that children and animals are more drawn to you during your period too, as they are picking up on your nurturing energies. Selene and Arianrhod arc both Mother moon goddesses, so read up about them and attune with their energies during your period.

Crone cycle: waning moon to dark moon

If your period falls on or between the waning and dark moon, you have a Crone or Dark Goddess cycle. Your moon-time powers are especially strong and will lean towards protection, divination and prophecy, as well as spells to increase knowledge and power. This is the phase of the wise woman, and you may find that you read a lot more during your moon time, particularly books on magic and witchcraft or that otherwise expand your mind. Women with this cycle tend particularly to crave solitude and are the most likely to experience prophetic dreaming. Hecate, Circe, the Morrigan and Morgan le Fay are all goddesses associated with this phase, so try to spend some time learning about them and attuning with their energies.

Whichever goddess cycle you are in, recognising it and learning to use its power is a key element in realising your feminine wisdom. Read all you can about the types of goddess associated with your current cycle and about periods in general, particularly those books written about the sacredness of menstruation. One book I feel every woman should read is *Moon Days: creative writings about menstruation* by Cassie Premo Steele. It will make you laugh, cheer for womankind and look at menstruation in a new and empowered way.

Moon time and divination

A woman's intuitive powers are greatly enhanced during her period. Many women experience vivid dreams during this time and find that they are more perceptive and aware of the spirit world, perhaps experiencing visitations from loved ones who have passed over. To witches, this heightened awareness is a gift to be utilised to the fullest, and it is traditional to practise some form of divination during moon time, when it may be easier and more accurate. This can also be a good time to learn a new divination tool.

Certain divinatory tools are more suited to moon time than others. Those that allow space for psychic journeying are the best, as they are not constrained by boundaries, so any form of scrying, automatic writing or psychometry is ideal. At this time avoid tools that are limited in their use, such as the pendulum, yes/no stones or oracular cards. Never use a ouija board at any time in your cycle, as this is an unsuitable tool for new practitioners and can lead to frightening experiences.

Scrying is the art of gazing into an object and seeing visions. It is particularly suitable for moon time, firstly because at this phase in your cycle you are already open and susceptible to visions, and secondly because the three main scrying tools (the crystal ball, the magic dark mirror, and pools of water) are all representations of the moon. Using these tools will strengthen your natural link to the moon, its magic and enchantment.

Scrying takes practice, and you will need to put in a lot of time and effort to master it. The visions will often appear in your mind's eye to begin with, rather than in the scrying vessel itself. As you become more practised, however, you may get an external vision within the tool. The first sign of an incoming external vision is when the crystal or mirror seems to fill with clouds or smoke. At this point most new witches are so shocked and surprised that they jump back and so break their concentration, thus missing out on the vision! Getting beyond this stage is perhaps the most difficult part of scrying. You must learn to focus and not let your concentration wander for a moment or the vision will be lost to you. Practice is the key to success.

Automatic writing is a way of contacting the spirit world. It is easy to do but, again, you will need to practise to reach any level of competence. All you need is a pencil and a pad. Hold the pencil loosely and place the point ready on the pad. Now close your eyes and concentrate. Soon you will feel the pencil begin to move. Don't break your concentration and keep your eyes closed. Continue for as long as you are comfortable and then look to see what you have written, or perhaps drawn. Keep a special note book for this purpose and practise often.

Psychometry is the art of picking up details about a place or person by touching objects connected to them. This is quite a flexible skill and can be used to learn about a particular person, living or dead, or about the past of an old building. In this form of divination the details will come to you as words, images, emotions or descriptions, which you must then relate to what you already know about the place or person, so building up a more detailed picture. Here's an example. Some years ago, a friend was showing me a collection of art cards that she had bought from a local artist in Cornwall. As I took hold of a card I had a strong vision of a mature, kind-faced man, painting at an easel. I described this image to my friend, down to the kind of clothes he wore, and she confirmed that I had described the artist perfectly. This is psychometry, and it is similar to a premonition in that, as in this instance, it can happen when you least expect it.

Practise by visiting old buildings and see what you pick up. Or visit antique stores and see if you get any flashes or images connected with the items within. Jewellery is always good for practising psychometry, as it is so personal. You can also practise this skill in the natural world around you, using it to determine the state of health of a tree or plant, or to tune in to the mood of an animal. Simply lay your hands gently upon the tree or animal and focus. What energies are you picking up? What do your psychic skills tell you? The more you practise psychometry, the more skilled you will become, and you will be able to apply this magical technique to many areas of your life.

As you can see, your period is a most magical time and the natural power boost it gives you can be utilised for divination in a number of ways. Try to make sure you tap into this power during your next cycle, as to ignore your period is to deny the sacred spirit of womanhood.

A moon-time temple

Throughout the centuries women have been conditioned to believe that periods are some kind of curse and that they are dirty. In older patriarchal societies the segregation of women from the rest of the clan during their moon time was sometimes enforced because menstruating women were considered to be unclean – a twisted version of the willing retreat into the menstrual lodge and its moon-time sisterhood practised in more female-friendly societies. Perhaps this enforced segregation had something to do with menfolk's fear of the vast power of menstruating women.

With more stress and responsibilities than ever before, modern women are in desperate need of a place to take a little time out and experience peace and calm during their moon time. Perhaps we should learn a lesson from our ancestors and insist on a little time to ourselves during menstruation. At the very least this should help to ease irritability caused by having to interact with others when you'd really much rather be left alone. Now, I'm not saying that your life should be put on hold every

28 days, but wouldn't it be easier to get through a busy day if you knew you had a couple of hours of quiet time to look forward to? And wouldn't that quiet time be even more appealing if you had a special place where you could relax, listen to soothing music, use massage oils to ease the cramps, meditate, read, write a diary and utilise your moon-time power by working a little magic or divining the future? Wouldn't your period be easier to deal with if you could enter a sacred moon-time temple? Unfortunately, the NHS doesn't provide such a thing, so you will have to create your own!

Have all your moon-time temple equipment ready before your period starts, as you may not feel like a shopping trip if you're experiencing cramps and so on – and this should be a fun activity! Your moon-time temple should be in a quiet room, so your bedroom is ideal. It should also be disposable, so you can clear it away after your period.

Begin by investing in a red voile bed canopy – this will form the 'womb' of your temple. It should be hung above the bed if possible. Alternatively, hang it over a comfy chair or in a quiet corner with lots of red cushions or tactile fabrics piled on the floor underneath. After your period, the canopy can be folded and stored in a drawer or cupboard, and all that will remain is the hook in the ceiling. Your moon-time temple should be a private thing.

Once the canopy is in place, continue to create the atmosphere of a temple. Use red velvet throws and scatter cushions to encourage relaxation, light lots of red candles and dot them about the room, and burn geranium essential oil or incense to fill your temple with a healing fragrance – geranium is renowned for its ability to ease the symptoms of PMT and period pains. Light the candles of your lunar altar and spend a little time here communing with one of the deities of your goddess cycle. Place a special item on this altar to acknowledge that this is your moon time – a red rose, a carnelian crystal, a red heart-shaped candle or trinket box. Anything red and feminine is appropriate.

Set up a little table or tray with items that will encourage self-love, such as a moon-time journal, a vase of red roses, a box of chocolates, a rose quartz crystal (to bring loving energies to your temple space), a great book about menstruation, a fabulous novel and so on.

If possible, make sure your temple is set up before your period starts so that it's all ready for you. Then take at least two hours to yourself every day for the duration of your moon time. Hang a 'Do not disturb' sign on the door, light the candles and incense, play soft music and throw on a comfy night dress. Work some magic if you wish or perform a divination, then lie on your bed, pulling the temple canopy around you to give a womb-like feeling, and relax. Read, write, meditate, take a nap and enjoy your special time alone.

Moon time symbols

Many women like to treat themselves during their moon time, and there are lots of meaningful ways to do this. Certain items are regarded by witches as moon-time symbols. By wearing one or having one around during your period, you will be constantly reminded of your moon time and your vast feminine power – while the significance of the symbol won't be obvious to anyone else.

You might like to buy yourself a bunch of red roses or some scented red candles each month to help create your moon-time temple. A bottle of deep-red tonic wine will help to keep your iron levels balanced, and you could choose to sip a glass of this as you relax in your temple. You might like to purchase a special red dress, long, loose and flowing, or a red satin nightdress to wear in your moon-time temple. Alternatively, invest in a pretty red garter to symbolise not only your moon time but also your power as a witch, as red garters were worn by witches in the past. You can wear the garter all day, and only you will know that you are honouring your sacred spirit of womanhood and feminine power. A pair of crescent moon earrings or a crescent moon brooch could be worn to the same effect, as could an item of jewellery studded with garnets (to represent your flow) or pearls (to represent the moon). Use your imagination and find a way to acknowledge your power and honour this special aspect of womanhood.

Moon-time journal

Writing a moon-time journal is a great way to keep track of how your menstrual cycle affects you. For most women, some months are worse than others, so making a note of any PMS you've had and period pains you've experienced can help you to see if there is a pattern and so be better prepared. Make a note of clumsy days, too, so that you are forewarned of when it's better to stay out of the best china cupboard!

Writing a journal is also a healthy way to release any anger or depression you may be feeling. Writing down your emotions helps you to process them and could prevent you from biting someone's head off!

Record any dreams, visions or visitations you've had, as well as magic you've worked and divinations you've done during your period. This will help you to see how menstruation enhances your powers as well as charting your magical progress in general.

Invest in a pretty red note book and a special pen. This will be your moon-time journal from now on, and you should keep it with your temple equipment. Write in it each month, hold nothing back, and soon it will become like an old friend.

The end of moontime – becoming a crone

In witchcraft, the crone, or post-menopausal woman, is respected and regarded with a certain amount of awe. She is the wise older woman who's been there, done that and lived to tell the tale, and so can pass on what she has learned. She is the elder, the living representative of the Dark Mother, and she teaches us that mature women are a force to be reckoned with. The elder tree is sacred to the Crone, so you might like to plant one in your garden to symbolise this new you. Alternatively, you could drink elderberry wine to celebrate the change and so embrace the wisdom and power that goes with it.

For many women in our society, menopause is a turbulent and traumatic time. As in puberty and pregnancy, your body is going through major changes. Mood swings, hot flushes and hormonal fluctuations may all be a part of this transition. On a psychological level, it can be difficult to accept this daily reminder that you are getting older, especially in a culture that values youth above all else. Even if you welcome the ending of your monthly cycle, it can still be difficult to accept that your body is no longer fertile.

The fact that your body is no longer capable of giving birth to a child does not mean that you are no longer fertile and nurturing in the wider sense. It is at this time of life that many women begin to fertilise and live their dreams, writing a first novel, setting up a business enterprise, learning a new skill or throwing themselves into an artistic pursuit. Some women take great pleasure in their grandchildren, enjoying all the fun without the hassles, while others choose to care for animals instead.

It is often assumed that after menopause a woman's sexuality goes into decline. This is not necessarily so. Menopause can increase your sexual drive, leaving you feeling more adventurous and liberated. Certain aspects of the Dark Mother, such as Morgan le Fey, have strong temptress energies. You may find that this kind of energy now comes to the fore, and you can indulge it without the fear of an unplanned pregnancy, so don't be surprised if you suddenly begin to feel your natural sexiness and allure!

Menopause is a natural progression. Embrace this new aspect of the Goddess as you move into the realm of wise women and elders. Use the power you have developed and the life lessons you have learned to move your life forward, making sure that you have lots of fun along the way. You are all power, all wisdom and definitely all woman – enjoy yourself!

As you can see, the moon has a profound effect on women's lives, both physically and spiritually. No other planet affects us in quite the same way, and understanding this unique and magical relationship is one of the key aspects in becoming a dedicated witch and a powerful wise woman.

Temptress

I turn the head of every man;
I capture any heart.
My role is but to tempt and tease,
And with skill I play my part.
I feel your eyes upon me;
I hear words unsaid;
I know you long to come with me
Where angels fear to tread.
You long to wind your fingers
In the tresses of my hair.
You are taunted by the challenge
Held within my tempting stare.
You yearn to kiss my ruby lips,
Feel the smoothness of my skin,
To hold me tightly in your arms
And breathe my fragrance in.
You wonder if you've been bewitched,
If you're the victim of my spell.
I'm in your every waking thought;
I'm in your dreams as well.
When you rock my hips with yours
And hear my sighs and cries,
You feel a state of ecstasy
And wonder if you've died.
But you forget I am the temptress;
Our love was never meant to last.
I was your femme fatale, you see,
And now our time is past.
And so you try to clip my wings;
Your love begins to smother.
I tell you so, and let you go,
And now I want another ...

Morgana

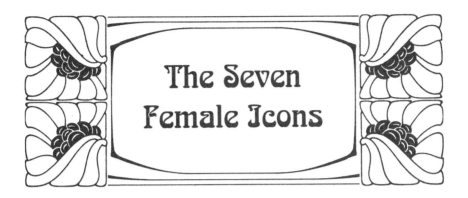

The Seven
Female Icons

So far we have looked at the basic structure and mechanics of witchcraft. Now we move on to discover the key to becoming an empowered woman in today's world: learning how to recognise your own source of feminine wisdom and redefine yourself as a woman.

Spells, rituals and sabbats are only part of what makes a witch. The true magic lies in her self-belief, independent spirit and indomitable power. By weaving all these things together you will come to know yourself on a deeper level and will radiate a sense of true power and wisdom. And with the knowledge and skills of magic at your fingertips, you will never be left without aid and protection when you need it, whatever troubles you may be facing.

In today's world there are so many images, both ancient and modern, of the feminine ideal that often our heads are spinning with thoughts of what we should and shouldn't be. Should we be soft and girly or a strong, sporty, ladette type? Should we be content to stay at home bringing up children or should we be on the fast track to a high-powered career? Should we seek out a lover and ensnare him with our Goddess-given charms or should we play by the rules and be coy, hoping that Mr Right will notice us? Should we wait to be rescued or should we rescue ourselves?

The simple answer is that we should be, are and can be all of the above! Each of the previous examples is but a small fragment of an ancient feminine archetype. There are seven of these female icons in all, and they are: virgin, temptress, mother, warrioress, enchantress, princess and queen. Both the high-powered career woman and the ladette are aspects of the warrioress. The ensnaring flirt is an aspect of the temptress, while her coy alter ego is an aspect of the virgin.

As you read through the following descriptions of the seven icons of womanhood, try to determine which you most identify with and can relate to. There may be more than one. Also notice which icons you can't relate to at all, the ones you barely recognise in yourself. There are no right and wrong answers. The point is to be completely honest with yourself. Note the icons you feel you really are, rather than the ones you would like to be! And don't worry. Each of these icons is present to some degree in every woman's character, although some will certainly be more prominent than others.

The virgin

To most people the term 'virgin' refers to someone who has never had sex, but there is also an older, more empowering interpretation of the word. In ancient times a virgin was a woman who was beholden to no man, needing no other, complete in herself. She was a strong and empowered individual who refused to be ruled by any masculine authority and who was fiercely independent.

Witches hold true to this older meaning of the word, by which we can all choose to be virgins if we want to, going our own way through life without the need of a male support system. And never has this ancient meaning of the word been more relevant to women! These days a woman has incredible freedom. She can have her own home, business, career, car and chosen lifestyle. She can even have children without a man in her life, and some women do actually choose to become single mothers. While a woman may opt to spend her life with a man, it is not essential to her wellbeing that she does so. In general, everything that a man can offer in material terms, a woman can obtain for herself.

The Virgin also denotes a state of innocence and purity, which for centuries has been linked to a lack of sexual experience. But does having sex mean that a woman is no longer pure? Of course not! Purity resides within the heart, the mind and the spirit, and it is up to the individual to maintain it. And sexually active women who retain a sense of their original innocence are very alluring indeed – good examples of this are Marilyn Monroe, Audrey Hepburn and even Kylie Minogue, who are all considered to be icons in their own right. Developing a sexy/sweet persona will increase your general magnetism, while maintaining a sense of innocence will help to keep your approach to life fresh and youthful. At the same time, considering yourself to be a virgin in the ancient sense will encourage independence and empowerment and can help you to work through any co-dependency issues you may have. It will help you to become a free spirit, ready to take on the world and all its challenges single-handed!

The Virgin strides boldly through life, seeing beauty in all things, finding joy wherever she goes. She is positive and proactive, and she always looks on the bright side. Although she is strong and independent, she is not without vulnerability. She sometimes trusts the wrong people, seeing truth where there is trickery, love where there is only dependence. However, her strength of spirit guides her through such trials and helps her to move forward in her life with grace and tenacity. The virgin doesn't believe in mistakes, only in lessons to be learned and joy to be had while learning.

To bring out your inner virgin, concentrate on her attributes and say the following charm three times:

Virgin hiding deep in me,
Finding strength in vulnerability,
Help me find joy in all that I do
And keep my ideals pure and true.
Needing no other, my spirit is free,
Complete in myself. So mote it be!

The temptress

You all know her ... she's the girl in the office who always looks great, the silver-screen siren you wish you could be, the sexy songstress adored by millions, the catwalk model strutting her stuff, the girl in the shopping mall turning heads, the barmaid pouring her smile into your boyfriend's drink, the ex your boyfriend will never forget ... She is the temptress – and she is everywhere!

The most successful temptress has a strong streak of the virgin running through her, for she knows that innocence is sexy. She bears her midriff and guards her heart, keeping any emotional vulnerabilities she may have firmly under wraps. She may offer the heady delights of no-strings sex or she may be merely flirtatious, but she is always fascinating and intoxicating.

The temptress is a female icon who both inspires and threatens us. We may want to be more like her, but we are quick to condemn any woman who openly flaunts her sexuality, especially if we are feeling vulnerable about our relationship or our own self-image. So just what is it about this archetype that provokes such contradictory reactions from us? There is no denying the power of sex, and if you have sex appeal then it stands to reason that you have a certain amount of power. The temptress oozes this power, and men flock to her in droves! This can be quite a threat if you are feeling less than tempting yourself!

But the temptress doesn't want to threaten women; she wants to teach us. Inside every woman is a temptress just waiting to be unleashed. She's the part of you that lusts after exotic perfumes, satin lingerie, scented candles and the latest shimmering shades of lip gloss. She urges you to sip champagne while relaxing in a hot bubbly bath, to read erotic fiction, to wear red lipstick and to put silk sheets on the bed. She encourages you to indulge in any kind of sensual pleasure that appeals to you, be this a full body massage, a dip in a hot tub or a home bath spa.

The temptress knows that all women can be sexy, regardless of age, weight or shape. She can teach you the skills of seduction, showing you not only how to capture the heart of a man, but also how to keep him. She knows that sexiness is about inner poise and outer confidence. It is in the way she pushes back her hair, throws her head back when laughing and looks up shyly yet knowingly through lowered lashes. It's in the way she casually strokes her throat, fingers the stem of her wine glass, walks across a room or pauses for a second in the doorway to let everyone see she's arrived. She was the inventor of body language and has the sexy/sweet persona down to a fine art.

She is also the femme fatale – the untouchable, unattainable creature who can capture a man's heart and mind in minutes and hold a piece of it forever. In this sense she is the old flame your husband will never forget, the one that got away, the one you are always secretly afraid will come back to haunt him, usurp you and ultimately lead him astray! In literature she is Helen of Troy, whose beauty began the Trojan war, or Guinevere taking Lancelot to be her lover, or even the Biblical Eve, flaunting her forbidden fruit!

The temptress is apparent in all aspects of modern-day life, taking her place on TV, CD, stage and screen. She is also seen working in offices, bars, clubs, restaurants, shopping centres and in any number of professions. She leaves a trace of exotic perfume in the air as she walks by, and she is always well dressed in a sexy, sassy way. Her bedroom is something of a boudoir, her drawers filled with beautiful night clothes and lingerie. She will spend her last few pence on a new lipstick and will trip through her day in a pair of killer heels. She takes responsibility for her own birth control, as she knows she will be the one left holding the baby! The temptress walks tall, proud of her allure and her sexual magnetism. She takes pleasure in herself, her body and her chosen partner – and she never fakes an orgasm!

Do you relate to the temptress? Can you see aspects of her within you? If your friends are always falling out with you because you can't stop flirting with their men, then maybe you need to tone down your temptress energies! On the other hand, if the idea of talking to a man leaves you wishing the ground would open up and swallow you, try saying this little charm three times daily to bring out your inner temptress:

> *Temptress with your will to please,*
> *I aim to tempt, I aim to tease.*
> *With your gifts I reel him in,*
> *Drawing power from within.*
> *Loving, kissing, flirting free,*
> *A femme fatale I now will be!*

The mother

The mother figure is predominant in society. We see her shopping for the family, doing the school run, tending the garden and also working in a full- or part-time job in some cases. She may be calm and collected or harried and stressed out, depending on how her particular day is going. She is a key figure in the world, and we can all relate to her in some way or another, for we were all born of a woman.

In witchcraft the Goddess is the Great Mother, nurturing and providing for us with complete generosity. She gently teaches us the lessons of life, in much the same ways that our earthly mother taught us the basic skills of survival. For some women the need to become a mother themselves is overwhelming – although this may not necessarily mean having a baby themselves. The need to mother may be directed towards animals and pets or it may be utilised in a career such as nursing, teaching or childminding. Any woman who works in the care industry is subconsciously tapping into the mother within.

Actively choosing to become the mother of a child takes a lot of courage. If the choice has been made and conception is difficult to achieve, a woman can feel lost, incomplete, and something of a genetic under-achiever. Part of the problem is that we live in a world where everything is available to us in an instant. We enjoy 24-hour shopping, fast food and instant access to the entire globe via the internet. We have become so accustomed to having everything we want 'Now!' that when we have to wait a while, we become fidgety and insecure. But nature is not like the local take-away. She works only to her own time schedule and will not be governed by human demands. Creating a brand-new life is a serious undertaking. You are asking your body to perform its greatest work of magic, so don't be surprised if it needs a little time to gear itself up for this!

On the other hand, some women actively choose to opt out of motherhood. The idea of going through a pregnancy and giving birth simply does not appeal to them. That we can make this choice is testimony to how far our gender has progressed. In the past, a woman was expected to bear as many children as her body could produce, often risking her own life in the process. Now, through the use of birth control, women can exercise their right not to have children, and such a choice should be respected.

Whether or not you decide to have children of your own, the mother icon is present within you, as it is within every woman. She is the side of you that enjoys cooking and home-making, that watches interior design programs and endeavours to create a beautiful living space. She guides you as you tend your garden and house plants. She is the part of you that gets angry at the thought of cruelty to children and animals, and that cries when your pet has to have a vaccination. And, ultimately, she is the force that inspires you to take care of those smaller or more vulnerable than yourself, be they animals, children, the elderly or those with learning disabilities. To help you to better understand your innate mothering instincts repeat the charm below three times:

> *Great Mother, hear this plea:*
> *Fill me with nurturing energy.*
> *Let me soothe and let me heal;*
> *Mother's love they now will feel.*
> *Peace and comfort I will give.*
> *Maternal instinct is your gift.*

The warrioress

The warrioress appears on the surface to be in total opposition to the mother icon. How can both these traits reside in any one woman? Well, they can and they do, because both these icons are born of the need to protect. It is the mother's job to nurture and protect, and this protection instinct is highly developed within the warrioress, where it becomes the need actively to defend. There are lots of stories about mothers performing incredible feats of strength in order to protect their child. These are actually classic examples of the warrioress at work. A woman can switch from mother to warrioress and back again in a matter of seconds.

Of course, in days gone by women were active warriors in their own right and would form armies, wear armour and go off to war like any man. In some cultures, notably that of the Celts, the women would fight alongside their menfolk, playing an equal part in the victory or defeat of their army. Warrior queens were both renowned and feared. Indeed, we have only to think of Boudicca, the Iceni queen, to realise that female warriors were once a force to be reckoned with. Even today women have important careers within the armed forces and the police and fire services, proving that this female need to protect is still prevalent within our society.

Modern women have a lot to thank the warrioress for. It is her energies that have moved mountains when it comes to matters of female equality and women's rights. This female icon was behind the suffrage and women's lib movements. She stands squarely against any form of abuse or sexual harassment and will cheer from the sidelines anything that serves to liberate and empower women further. Her energies can be found in any safe house for women who have suffered domestic violence, as she fills these survivors with hope, courage and the prospect of a better life.

Through the ages, the warrioress has supported such progressive moves as female education, jobs for women, equal pay and the development of effective contraception, which won back the ancient right of Thigh Freedom. She was responsible for putting an end to the man's world in which women were treated as second-class citizens. Echoes of the warrioress can also be seen in the rebirth of Goddess-oriented spiritualities, as they teach the sacredness of womankind. She opposes all crimes against women and children.

The warrioress takes everything in her stride. She is strong and independent. She is feisty, yet she remains cool-headed in conflict or crisis, and she is governed by her intellect as much as her emotions. She will fight to defend her rights, her family and loved ones, and her home. She will be an active participant in any movement that empowers or liberates womankind in any way, and she will use her strength to protect and comfort those sister women who have suffered at the hands of men.

The warrioress urges you to be on your guard at all times. She is the part of you that would love to learn kick-boxing or that takes up a male-dominated sport or career. She encourages you to excel at work, to carve out a career for yourself and to remain true to your ambitions regardless of what others may say. She also urges you to fit window locks and door chains to your home, and to carry out a quick security check every night before bed to make sure the house is secure.

She is constantly reminding you to strengthen your defences on an emotional level as well as a physical one – she doesn't want you to get hurt in any way. She pushes you to learn new skills that will increase your independence, such as driving a car, changing a wheel, camping and survival skills, and even using a computer. She helps you to attune with your warrior spirit by urging you to go horse riding, climbing, swimming, white water rafting or sailing. She inspires you to watch swashbuckling movies that teach a message of honour and valour.

When you are out shopping she reminds you of the practical things you need for your own defence, such as light bulbs for the outdoor security light, a personal alarm, a new lock for the garden shed or a stronger latch for the garden gate. She does all she can to keep you from harm's way, and she knows that the best defence is often self-reliance. The warrioress needs no man to rescue her; she is her own knight in shining armour, and she rescues herself!

To bring out your inner Warrioress repeat the following charm three times:

> *I need no man to rescue me;*
> *I set my warrior spirit free.*
> *I guard and protect all that is mine;*
> *I know when to draw the battle line.*
> *With courage and valour I stand my ground.*
> *With strength and honour victory is found!*

The enchantress

Who wouldn't want to be an enchantress? This is the female icon lots of women would like to attune with, changing their lives for the better with a few well-chosen words and a flick of the wrist. But, as we have already seen, magic is never that simple. It is a craft, a skill and an art. It takes dedication to become an adept practitioner of magic, and this is where this female icon can help you, for if you evoke your inner enchantress, you will find a latent ability just waiting to be utilised.

This icon is known by many names. Sorceress, priestess, witch and wise woman are all ways to describe her, and it is her magic that calls you home to the Craft right now. It was the voice of the enchantress that urged you to buy this book in the first place! This means that you have already forged a link with your inner enchantress, and your magical journey has already begun.

The enchantress exudes mystery and power. She plays her cards close to her chest and never tells all about herself – she always keeps a part of her life private. She likes to keep people guessing about herself and her plans. She is determined and very self-motivated. She knows that it is she alone who is responsible for making her life move forward and directing it towards the ultimate success of her goals. The enchantress is often very ambitious and is at her most powerful when coupled with the warrioress and the temptress – these three feminine icons working together within one woman can bring just about anything into being.

This icon knows the power of positive thinking

and is a great believer in 'fake it till you make it', which she can carry off with complete conviction. She sees the magic of nature all around her and loves getting out and about, regardless of the weather or the season. She likes her own company and craves solitude and space to work her magic, which fills every aspect of her life.

The enchantress teaches you to trust your instincts and to nurture your intuition. She blesses you with vivid and sometimes prophetic dreams and offers the gifts of knowledge and learning. She invites you to look up at the moon and see the magic it holds as well as the beauty, and she teaches you the sacredness of your moon time, offering natural remedies to ease the discomforts. Under her guidance you will learn to follow the movements of the planets and to recognise the constellations. She teaches that there is hidden power in all things and shows you how to tap into it.

It is this icon who urges you to become a bookworm, constantly questing for greater knowledge and wisdom. She urges you to buy a pack of Tarot cards or a crystal ball, to read your horoscope or to go and have your fortune told, as well as to create an altar, watch magical films and learn the medicinal uses of herbs. The enchantress is the part of you that burns oils, lights candles and invests in the tools of your magical trade. She covets that pewter goblet or that beautiful spirit board that will open up doors to the Otherworld. She teaches that you are a goddess in your own right and in your own way, and that true spirituality is within you and not out of your reach.

The Enchantress shows you that all you could wish for is yours for the taking, and she urges you to wish wisely and to make your life choices in an informed manner. To attune with your inner enchantress repeat the following charm three times:

Enchantress of magic, of witchcraft and spell,
I know you have wise woman's secrets to tell.
Teach me the spiral, the cycle, the dream;
Teach me to see the seen and unseen.
Show me the seasons, the tide's ebb and flow.
Moon magic and wisdom I wish now to know.

The princess

Most little girls go through a princess phase. For many this is left behind with the fairy-tales and broken dolls of childhood, but some women retain an aspect of the Princess persona, and this is no bad thing, for the Princess teaches us that we are someone extra-special, worthy of love, respect and adoration. Some women dream of finding a man who will treat them like a princess, but it's my belief that they're really looking for a man who will acknowledge that they already hold this female icon within them, and will honour and respect them accordingly.

The beautiful princess is in every fairy story, a corner stone of children's literature and folklore. She is kind and gentle, honest and

true, and when life doesn't go her way she shoulders her burdens and sings cheerfully through the drudgery. Though she acknowledges that life is sometimes unfair, she is never truly jaded by it, managing to maintain a purity of heart that we could all learn something from. She is never sarcastic or cynical, but strives to see the good in others and the opportunities within any given situation. She is the original Pollyanna, always looking for the silver lining within every cloud and focusing on the bright side of things.

The Princess teaches you that you are an exceptional and unique individual. You are a rare creature of grace and charm, and you have your own special talents. There is no-one quite like you anywhere, and your inner princess wants both you and the world to recognise and acknowledge that fact. She urges you to develop your personal talents and maintain a sense of individuality.

The princess encourages you to create a beautiful home for yourself and to fill each room with fresh flowers. She invites you to turn aspects of your life into the fairy-tale, whether this means growing climbing roses up the side of your house, or kissing a live frog and wishing for Mr Right! She is the side of you that longs to float through the day in a sweeping gown, to grow your hair as long as possible so you can spend hours brushing it out with a silver hair brush, or to buy a glass slipper or a berry-red cloak.

Your inner Princess longs to ride in a horse-drawn carriage or become a prima ballerina. She drives you to do all things girly, such as keeping a diary, wearing pink and pearls, watching romantic movies and singing along to your favourite pop princess. She keeps safe all your childhood dreams and ambitions and inspires you to re-read your favourite fairy-tales, seeing the deeper meaning hidden within them.

The Princess pirouettes through life smiling and singing. She knows that she is talented and special, that she is worthy of true love and that her inner beauty will always shine through. She knows that she deserves the good things in life and she believes in treating herself every now and then.

The Princess believes in true love and walks away from any relationship that disempowers her in any way, choosing instead to be single until the right man comes along – one who will respect her boundaries and honour her royal person. She holds her head high and mentally plays a royal fanfare whenever she enters a room!

To bring out your inner princess repeat the following charm three times:

> *A royal princess I would be,*
> *The picture of femininity.*
> *All who see me shall adore me;*
> *The world's finest gifts are heaped before me.*
> *Shining forth my inner beauty,*
> *I welcome those who show me fealty.*

The queen

When the princess matures, she ascends the throne and becomes the queen. In a sense, the queen is the princess with all the responsibilities of adulthood. As soon as a young woman leaves the parental home and becomes the ruler of her own household, she encounters this icon.

The queen demands loyalty and respect from those around her and presents a calm yet commanding presence. She rules over her domestic kingdom, and may exude her power in her chosen career too. Although she likes to be in charge, she also uses her power for the good of others and will offer shelter to those

in genuine need. She is fair and just, bountiful and benevolent, and she wields her power with elegance and grace, the picture of feminine dignity and poise. She is self-possessed and knows her own mind, refusing to bend to another's will, but she respects the different views held by different people and different cultures. The queen carries herself with decorum, exuding a sense of nobility and stateliness. She is loyal and faithful to her chosen partner and is unwavering in her personal beliefs. She is the steadfast matriarch of her family and puts the good of her clan before her personal wishes.

The queen teaches us to nurture our sense of nobility. She encourages us to shoulder our responsibilities with dignity, and she shows us that duty can be a reward in itself. At the same time, it is your inner queen who urges you to employ a cleaner or childminder (or who makes you dream of doing so) so that you can enjoy time to yourself and other good things. She loves to delegate and to be waited on, liking nothing more than to dine out or have clothes made especially for her. This icon will be strong within you if you work in a position of authority and have a team of people working under you.

This icon is the part of you that enjoys responsibility and dreams of living in a large house. It may urge you to become a lady of leisure or to devote yourself to your home and family, to philanthropy or to your chosen career. The queen will always make you stand out in a crowd – she wants your nobility to shine!

The queen icon may inspire you to buy a special chair for your use only, for every queen needs a throne to sit on. This could be a cosy armchair, a boudoir chair, a carved wooden rocking chair or even a glamorous chaise longue. The queen encourages you to sit regally upon your throne and dictate how your personal kingdom will be run.

This icon may also encourage you to define a trademark for yourself. In days of old, each queen had her own coat of arms and a personal sigil. Your inner queen may inspire you to wear a particular motif on your clothes or in the form of jewellery. My own trademark sigils are the Bruce coat of arms and the butterfly. I have lots of jewellery with a butterfly design, and clothes with tiny butterflies embroidered on them, while my Bruce coat of arms keyring goes with me everywhere. A woman I know is never seen without her token dragonfly somewhere about her person; this is certainly her trademark sigil.

You may already have a trademark sigil but have been unaware of it up to now. This is your inner queen making herself known! She instructs you to take hold of your power and use it well, to be the monarch of your own life and the queen of your own reality. She needs no crown or coronation to proclaim her majesty; she declares it herself, proudly flying her own royal standard! To bring out your inner Queen say the following charm three times:

> It is a queen that I would be,
> Declaring my own nobility.
> From my duty I will not shy;
> My royal standard I will fly.
> My regalness I do proclaim
> That all shall know my royal name!

Balancing the icons

In order to fully take back her power a woman must balance the seven female icons within her personality. Of course, we can all relate to some icons more than others, and there will be days when it serves us best to concentrate on the energies of one icon in particular. For example, if you were having to meet a lot of challenges at work, you might want to tune into your inner warrioress. In general, though, a woman is most powerful when she can acknowledge all these icons within her and tap into their various energies and powers.

It may be that you have more of one icon in you than the others. For example, if you tend to react with aggression, you may have too much of the warrioress in you. In this case, you need to work regularly with the mother aspect of your character to try to bring about a balance. If you are very shy, try working with the energies of the temptress; if you are feeling powerless, use the enchantress; if you feel invisible, tap into the princess or the queen; if you need to be more independent, call on the feisty virgin, and so on.

As there are seven icons, try to devote each day of the week to a different female aspect. Begin on a Monday with the virgin and tune into her energies within you. On Tuesday become the temptress, on Wednesday nurture your mother instincts, on Thursday be the warrioress, on Friday feel the power of the enchantress, on Saturday be a princess, and on Sunday become the queen. In this way you will come to know the icons intimately and will understand how they relate to you on a personal level – which you need to enhance and which you may need to tone down a little.

The trick is to include an equal measure of each of the icons within your personality so that you can be all that is best in womanhood on a daily basis. It will then be easier to bring one particular icon to the fore when you need its energy to face a particular challenge in life. This will take a little time and effort, but it is well worth doing, as you will feel more complete in yourself and more powerful as a result.

Warrioress

The spirit of Boudicca flows through me
As I embrace the battle light.
I do not fear death nor pain
But take on a warrior's might.
As ravens circle high above,
I whisper the Morrigan's name,
Ask for her blessings and call her love
And pray for battle fame.
A gentle breeze lifts my plaits
And cools woad-painted skin.
I slam my sword against my shield
And begin the battle din.
So it begins as arrows fly.
The enemy sound the advance.
I raise my shield as arrows rain,
And dodge the point of a lance.
I step and turn, my sword upraised,
And scream my battle cry.
I cut and thrust, rip and tear,
For to kill is not to die.
So it goes on from dawn till dusk,
And the battlefield runs red.
My heart is frozen; all I feel
Is the battle rage in my head.
My eyes see through a crimson haze
As the sun begins to set,
Echoing the battle field,
Where the challenge has been met.
Breathing deep I look around;
We have crossed the battle line.
The Morrigan has smiled on us,
And victory is ours – this time.

Morgana

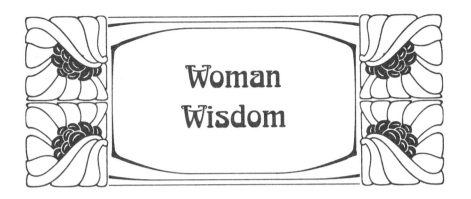

Woman Wisdom

To take back fully your power as a woman it is vital that you see yourself as a individual and a person in your own right. You are so much more than wife, daughter, mother, sister, friend, employee and so on. You have a unique set of talents and gifts that you can tap into, and you deserve to have time and space to yourself, as well as your own friends and interests outside of work or family.

So many women live their lives for other people, constantly trying to please friends and family members and fit in with everyone else's plans and schedules. This kind of behaviour can leave you feeling stressed and taken for granted, and waging a constant battle against time – there never seems to be enough of it. If all this sounds familiar, you need to recognise that it is impossible to please everyone all of the time and learn to say no occasionally. Stand your ground and remember to please yourself once in a while.

Gaining a sense of independence can sometimes be an uphill struggle for women, and unfortunately no-one is going to hand it to you on a silver platter. Independence is something that you must take. You must carve it out of your life yourself. If you wait for someone to give you more space, you'll be waiting a long time.

So how does a woman go about creating her independence? If you live alone, you're half way there already, because you are managing your life solo. Nevertheless, you still need to be able to show people where your boundaries are. If you don't like surprise visits, for example, insist that people telephone first to ensure that your guests arrive at a time that is convenient to you. You may also like to turn your phones off once in a while so that you can spend a few blissfully uninterrupted hours of quality alone time.

Fortunately, being single is now recognised as a viable personal life choice, but this doesn't always save single girls from the well-meaning pity of others, who assume that single life must be both boring and lonely. It is anything but! In general, a single girl has less demands on her time, so she can enjoy herself to the fullest. It could just be that those who lavish their pity on you are in reality envious of your singleton lifestyle and are trying to hide their jealousy and dissatisfaction with their own life.

These days more people are opting to stay within the parental home for longer, to the point where people in their twenties and even thirties are still living at home with their mum and dad. The fact that house prices have escalated over the last decade or so is partly to blame for this current trend, as it has put many properties – and even entire areas – beyond the reach of the average first-time buyer. But renting is always an option and should be seriously considered if you want to achieve a state of full independence and the self-respect that goes with it.

It is said that to some extent you will always be treated like a child while living with your parents, and this can be incredibly frustrating. But even in such circumstances, you must begin to set your boundaries and claim your independence. The busier you are, the less time you will spend under parental scrutiny. Take charge of your own laundry and make sure you prepare your own meals as often as possible. If this means dining out, then so be it. Go to a friend's or boyfriend's for dinner, or even to a pizza place. Demonstrate your independence by doing things alone – go to the cinema by yourself, take a weekend trip alone or book a table for one in your favourite restaurant. Don't tell all about your life. Play your cards a little close to your chest. There's no need to be secretive or dishonest, but be vague when questioned and then politely change the subject. If pressed, insist on your right to privacy.

Maintaining a sense of independence when in a relationship can often be even more difficult, especially if you have children to take care of. But it is essential to preserve some time for yourself. Try not to lose touch with your friends. Spending an evening out with your girlfriends will help you to keep a sense of yourself as an individual, and a little time away from your partner will ensure that you appreciate one another more. When the kids are at school, take at least one day to yourself and go out to lunch, either by yourself or with a friend. Go and see a matinée at the theatre, have a facial or a manicure or go for an afternoon drink or a walk in the park. Take up a sport or a hobby. Do something that is totally unrelated to your family, something that is just for you. Most importantly, try to retain at least one aspect of your single life – this could be going horse riding, dancing or ice skating, or perhaps belonging to a writer's circle or reading group. Whatever you did regularly as a single girl, keep doing it! This will remind you that you are a person in your own right, with your own hobbies and interests, and that you still exist outside the relationship and motherhood!

Whatever your current circumstances may be and however you choose to define your own independence, begin to establish your boundaries immediately. People will probably be surprised at first, particularly if you have always tried to please everyone else in the past, and they may get a little huffy. But stand your ground and defend the boundaries you have laid down. Remember, independence is something you create for yourself, and you must defend it constantly or it will be steadily chipped away by the

demands of others. Tell yourself daily that you are an independent woman and that you will not let anyone encroach on that independence. Take back your power and gain the space you need to live the life you want.

Defining your personal woman's wisdom

Each woman's wisdom is different from that of her sisters, because it comes from the core of her being. Native American Indians have a saying that goes, 'This is my truth', which basically means, 'This is who I am; this is how I see the world and myself within it.' Our woman's wisdom is our own truth, one that we must each define for ourselves and which will change and develop over time as we progress through life.

Defining your own truth or woman's wisdom, will help you to have a deeper understanding of yourself and how you relate to the world in general. It will show you who you are at your deepest level and can guide you to your true purpose in life. Some women feel swept away by life and overwhelmed by the demands society places upon them. Women today may well have it all, but this usually goes hand in hand with doing it all too! By stripping away unwanted influences on our lives, we come to see who we really are and what is holding us back.

It is vital that you remain positive when defining your woman's wisdom. It should represent all that is wonderful about you, all that is fascinating, all that is unique. It should be a testament to your individuality and it should sing your praises. This is no time to be overly modest! Take a pad and a pen and begin to define your personal woman's wisdom. If it takes you a while to get started, just keep asking yourself who you really are – eventually something will come. A poetic description of your appearance is always a good starting point and should help to get the ball rolling. Think of a suitable title for your poem and keep a copy of it on your altar or by your bed. Read it every day to give you a a boost.

This is a woman's wisdom poem based upon my own truth:

Butterfly Song

My spirit is that of the butterfly.
My beauty is that of the night.
My skin is ivory and satin-smooth.
My eyes hold a secret in their chestnut gleam.
Raven-dark tresses fall to my hips.
My smile is a radiant moonbeam.
The blood of Clan Bruce flows through my veins.
The grace of the Goddess lives in my heart.
The voice of the witch speaks through my lips.
The scent of the Wild Wood resides in my hair.
The force of the mountains strengthens my might.
The heat of the sun echoes my passion.
I am a wordsmith, an author and poet.
I am an equestrienne and rider of steeds.
I am a priestess of the Great Goddess.
I am an enchantress of magic and spell.
I am a needlewoman, stitching my standard.
I am a warrioress defending my home.
I am steadfastly loyal to my loved ones.
I sing with the voice of a siren.
I dance with the grace of the breeze.
I read with the hunger of a starving mind.
I live with the truth of my dreams.
I weave my own destiny.
I create my own path.
I am true to myself.
I am fiercely independent.
I am determined and resourceful.
I am feisty and strong-willed.
I am fragile and vulnerable.
I try to be fearless.
Yet still I am a butterfly.
This is my woman's wisdom.
This is my truth.

Your own poem of woman's wisdom may be
similar or it may be very different.
Remember to include your talents,
gifts and virtues and to make it all
very positive. This poem is a
celebration of you. No-one else need
ever see it, but in acknowledging your
own uniqueness in this way and reading
through the poem often yourself, you will
start to feel more empowered and worthy of
all that the universe has to offer – for you are a
wise woman and you deserve to be happy!

It's all in the name

In magical terms, names have power. In the past it was thought that
to know someone's name was to have a certain amount of power
over that person. This could be the reason for bestowing more than
one name on a child, and the reason we are often shy about
revealing our middle name if we have one.

How we relate to our name is important. Our given name isn't
something we have any control over, of course. However, a
nickname can be a way of expressing ourselves, stamping our
personality on the world and taking our place within our chosen
circle of friends. Sometimes these names stick with us into our
adult lives. My best friends still call me Maz, while my mother calls
me Marianna – this is her special name for me and no-one else ever
uses it. My magical name is Morgana, and I have a secret spirit
name too, known only to myself and the universe.

What does your name mean to you? Do you like it? Do you use a
shortened version or a nickname instead? If you have always
disliked your name, think about changing it. Or if you are sick of
being called by a shortened version, insist that people use your full
name. Simply refuse to answer them or acknowledge them in any
way until they have addressed you as you would wish. This may at

first seem rather rude, but it is an excellent way of getting your point across, and eventually people will start to call you by the name of your choosing.

Remember your surname too. Your surname of birth is your link with your family and ancestors on one side. I love being a Bruce because I understand the history and the heritage that the name carries. I am proud of my surname and strive to live up to it. But perhaps you feel differently about your own surname. If you are divorced you might prefer to revert to your maiden name, rather than carrying around the baggage of a dead relationship. I personally feel that a woman should keep her own name through marriage, rather than assuming the identity of her husband. Be aware that this option is open to you.

Finally, most witches choose a magical name for themselves. This is the name that they use when in the magic circle. It refers to their own witch persona and it is one that makes them feel magical and powerful. If you decide to use a magical name, you might pick one from mythology or literature, such as Artemis, Circe, Ceres, Guinevere, Arwen or Bathsheba. Or you could look to nature for inspiration and come up with Moon Maiden, Silver Swan, Rainbow, Blossom or Meadow. Choose your magical name with care and then write it in the front of your Book of Shadows.

As you can see, your name is a key component in how you view yourself and how you identify with society in general, so try to make sure it serves you well. You should be completely happy with all the names you are known by, in all aspects of your life. If you are not, take the necessary steps to make a change. As a result you will become a whole new you!

The witch's cloak of empowerment

A witch's cloak is her mantle of power. It may be a real garment or it may be a simple visualisation technique that increases her sense of self-confidence and power. In this aspect, it can be worn any time, any place, anywhere!

Lots of witches have a special cloak that they wear to add a sense of occasion to a ritual or a gathering of like-minded friends. They may also wear their cloak when they are feeling introspective or vulnerable. We all have times when the day seems to lie heavy upon our shoulders; you may find that wrapping yourself in your witch's cloak for a while offers comfort and a sense of magical protection. Used in this way, the witch's cloak envelops you in the magic of the Craft and reminds you of your power. And, in practical terms, your cloak can keep you warm when you are working outdoor magic in the chill of the night. But what about those occasions when wearing a real witch's cloak is out of the question? Well, then you put on an imaginary garment, an

ethereal cloak of confidence and empowerment. Most people are familiar with the concept of wearing a 'mask' of some sort. We do this when, for example, we 'put on a brave face' during times of stress or bereavement. The imaginary witch's cloak takes this idea a step further, creating a visualised cloak that can be used to empower the witch in any number of situations.

The cloak is worn on a regular basis until we have absorbed its gift into our personality. For example, if you suffer from shyness, you might imagine that you wear a cloak of total confidence and self-assurance. By wearing this cloak on a daily basis for a period of time, you will eventually become more confident. By using the witch's cloak you can effectively become anything you want to be. If you would like to be a bit of a temptress, create a cloak of sexy siren energy. If you would like to feel happier in yourself, create a cloak of joy, and so on. The witch's cloak is also a great way to attune with the seven icons of womanhood that we looked at in the last chapter. Visualise a cloak that represents each of the icons in turn and imagine yourself wearing it. This will help you to bring out your inner princess, warrioress, enchantress and so on.

There is no limit to the ways in which you can use this visualised cloak, and it will enable you to change anything about your personality you don't like. With a little effort, you will eventually become the kind of person you have always wanted to be! Just take things slowly and work through one step at a time, visualising your magical cloak of empowerment in any way you choose.

Perfecting a persona

Another technique I have found especially empowering is that of creating and perfecting an entire persona. We see examples of this all the time when we watch celebrities – often there is a distance between the person they really are and the creature they portray on stage or screen. They have created a persona for themselves in order to protect their personal space and privacy, and also to ensure that the world sees them in a particular way. This is similar to wearing the visualised magical cloak, but a persona is far more detailed and is usually a close representation of a personal ideal.

Creating a persona is also a great way to 'fake it till you make it'. If you dream of being a published writer, then create the persona of a successful author. If your ambition is to be a wealthy entrepreneur, create that persona for yourself and act as if you were already living your dream.

This technique is actually a form of sympathetic magic, for like attracts like, and in acting out a particular persona you will magnetise the lifestyle you truly want to live. Eventually your chosen persona will cease to be an act and will become who you really are. In creating a persona we are hiding our vulnerabilities and showing only our strengths. We can use our chosen persona to move forwards in our life, to raise our self-esteem, to overcome faults and bad habits, and even as a means of defence. We can change our persona at will if necessary, adopting a new one as we grow and evolve and our needs change. And we can use the persona to take charge of our image – not only the image we portray to the outside world but our-self image too, which is perhaps more important.

But where does a witch find inspiration for her persona and how do you go about creating one for yourself? Well, personas are all around us – on TV, in books, walking down the high street of your home town ... All you need to do is decide what type of persona would serve you best at this time in your life and begin to create it. You might choose one that will move you forward in life and take you towards your ultimate ambitions and career goals, for example the persona of a successful businesswoman, an artist or a dancer. Your persona might be used to overcome a fault or negative thought pattern. For example, if you feel inadequate about the way you look, create the persona of a supermodel or a film star. This will eventually enable you to shine in your own right. Fairy-tales are a great place to find a persona, for example the white witch, the fairy godmother and the princess. You can, of course, use any of the female icons as your persona.

In some instances a persona can be used to protect yourself and to withdraw from life a little. If you have been badly hurt in the past and need to protect your heart for a while to give yourself the necessary time to heal, try adopting an ice maiden persona. This will protect you from those who do not have your best interests at heart, while anyone truly worth knowing will take the time to look beyond the superficial frostiness and see the light and warmth beneath. This is a very powerful form of defence will give you the space you need to get back on your feet after a romantic disappointment or other life trauma.

Creating a persona

Once you have chosen your ideal persona, you need to do a little work to create it. You will need a pad and a pen and a few moments of peace and quiet. Now write the name of your chosen persona at the top of the page, for example 'Snow Queen'. Beneath it write down anything that relates to this character. You can use key words, full sentences or phrases. Here is an example:

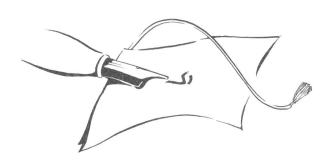

Snow Queen

Ice maiden.
Frosty, cool, icy, strong.
Determined, unfeeling, cold, hard.
Piercing stare.
Silver, white, icy-blue.
Distant, unattainable.
Made of glass, fragile, delicate as a snow flake.
Sharp, cutting as an icicle.
Shimmering, sparkling.
Beautiful yet untouchable.
Frost bite.
Can be shattered, can be melted.

In writing out your persona in this way, you will begin to see all her various facets and so develop a blueprint. Once you have the blueprint, it becomes easy to adopt the persona for yourself, by acting the way she would act, wearing the colours that we associate with her and so on. This works for any persona you wish to use, be it a supermodel or a businesswoman.

Now begin to incorporate the persona into your daily life. Ask yourself questions such as:

◆ What would the snow queen wear to this occasion?
◆ How would the snow queen deal with this situation?
◆ What decision would the snow queen reach on this matter?
◆ How would the snow queen behave with this person?

Asking yourself these simple questions in your daily life will help you to maintain your chosen persona on a daily basis. It may feel strange at first, but you will soon become accustomed to acting out your new role, and eventually it will become second nature. You will have adopted your chosen persona completely, creating a powerful life tool.

Radiance, mystery and allure

All women have radiance, mystery and allure, but only a few know how to tap into these feminine qualities and bring them to the fore of their personality. In fact, some women will go so far as to deny that they could ever be radiant or alluring!

Of course, we all have days when we feel anything but radiant, are far too busy to be mysterious and simply too tired to be alluring. But that doesn't mean that these qualities are not lying dormant within you; it simply means that they need waking up! In this section we will be giving your feminine qualities of radiance, mystery and allure a wake-up call.

Developing your inner radiance

Radiance is an inner glow that will make you shine! Brides, expectant mothers and women in love are all often described as radiant, because the incredible joy they are feeling radiates out into the world and so affects other people. When you are radiant, you will attract people into your circle. Friends, family members, lovers ... everyone will want to be near you. Strangers will smile at you, nod at you or even strike up a conversation. Radiance is magnetic, and it will turn you into the star attraction. And if you are having a bad day, tuning in to your natural radiance will help you to deal with any difficulties and find some degree of joy in every aspect of your life.

So just what is it that makes a person radiant? It is a combination of joy, love and a sense of achievement. Finding something each day to be joyful about is the first step to developing your radiance. Often joy can be found in the simplest things – a relaxing bubble bath, the unexpected appearance of a rainbow or the purring of your cat as you stroke him. Actively looking for a source of joy each day will make you feel good about your life and generally more positive.

Love is all around us, and acknowledging this fact can develop your radiance too. Be aware of the love of family, friends, partner, children – anyone who is close to you. Pets also offer love, and their loyalty is unquestionable. But the most important kind of love for developing radiance is self-love. Learn to love and accept yourself just as you are and know that you are a remarkable woman. You are a unique and beautiful person, and you have something worthwhile to offer this world. Be content with who you are and work on improving what you have – so that you love yourself even more.

Which brings us to another source of radiance: achievement. A sense of achievement in what you do will help you to feel good about yourself and will give your life purpose and meaning. Achievements need not be huge to be significant. Making it through a full working week can be an achievement, as can doing a job around the house that you've been putting off. Anything that keeps the house running smoothly, the kids organised or your career on track is an achievement. Then, of course, there are the bigger achievements: passing a driving test or an exam, signing up for a study course or educational class, doing a workout, getting a promotion at work, becoming a parent and so on. We all achieve lots and lots of things every day. The trick is to learn to acknowledge these achievements, be they large or small. This will increase your positivity and enhance your natural radiance.

Each morning as you begin your day, think joy, love and achievement. Progress through your day experiencing and acknowledging these emotions and your radiance will begin to shine through.

And while you're waiting for your natural radiance to make you sparkle, here are a few tips to gain the artificial variety:

- ◆ Use a shampoo that makes your hair really shine, or use a special shine serum after shampooing.
- ◆ Use eye drops designed to make your eyes sparkle.
- ◆ Use a whitening toothpaste to make your teeth gleam.
- ◆ Smile and laugh as often as possible.
- ◆ Think happy thoughts as often as you can.

Developing your inner mystery

Everyone loves a good mystery! And a woman who is in tune with her own sense of mystery will captivate just about anyone. By developing an aura of mystique, you will make yourself more attractive and interesting to others. Thinking of yourself as a multi-faceted individual will increase your inner mystery, as you will project a three-dimensional personality of great depth. Mysterious women are seldom accused of being shallow and superficial. And mystery is definitely part of being a witch!

Begin to see yourself as a woman of mystery. Play your cards close to your chest, be a little vague when asked about yourself and your life and avoid telling anyone everything there is to know about you. Preserve a secret self, a part of you that nobody else knows about. This secret could be a pole dancing class you're taking, a hidden tattoo or even a secret lover. It could be as simple as your love of moonlit woodland walks at midnight or your involvement in the Craft itself – but whatever it is it should be something that is only for you.

Another way to develop your mystique is to try to live from moment to moment. This may be difficult if, like me, you prefer to have things organised at least a week in advance. But occasionally it's nice to twist the schedule a little out of shape or to shake things up entirely and see where they land. Living in the moment will encourage you to take more pleasure in your day and will definitely increase your mystique as even you won't know in advance what you'll be up to next! And surprising yourself is often the greatest surprise of all.

Keeping a journal that no-one else reads will develop your mystery too. Having a special place where you can write down all your thoughts, feelings, fears and so on enables you to come to understand yourself on a profound level and to live from your mysterious deeps. A woman who keeps a diary is automatically mysterious to others, as everyone will be curious what and who you're writing about! Don't let anyone read your diary, but let it be known that you are writing one – this will set everyone wondering!

Use these simple tricks to help you cultivate your mystery:
◆ Develop a Mona Lisa smile.
◆ Create a secret self.
◆ Work magic by moonlight.
◆ For one day don't make any plans and just see what happens.
◆ Day-dream and lose yourself in secret thoughts!

Developing your allure

Allure is the ultimate form of sensuous sexuality. It is provocative and sexy without being brazen or inappropriate. Women with allure are fascinating individuals who can ensnare both men and women with their charm. Alluring women are appealing and have a strong sense of their own desirability. Their eyes are full of an unspoken promise. They know that they are sexy, no matter what they wear or what dress size they happen to be. And they know that they don't need to bear all to be alluring – they understand the truth of hidden mysteries! They wear outfits that suit them and enhance their womanly curves, rather than flaunting too much flesh!

To develop your natural allure you need to learn to see yourself as a desirable and exciting woman. Dressing well will turn heads, and this will reinforce your self-belief. Work on your movement too. Alluring woman tend to move slowly and gracefully, as if they have all the time in the world. Try walking in a slow seductive manner and use the model's trick of imagining a white line painted on the floor like a tightrope. Balance your steps on this imaginary line as you walk. This will give you the classic model walk, with a sexy stride and swaying hips. Walk tall and keep your head up. Also, try to imitate the graceful movements of the cat, bringing a feline elegance to your body language.

Read books about body language so that you can control what subtle signals you're giving out and interpret those of other people. Take an exercise or dance class so that you are more aware of your body and how it moves. Read books about the art of flirting and practise the skills they teach whenever you can. Develop your inner poise and self-confidence.

Another way to enhance your natural allure is to indulge in sexy fantasies. Think about Brad Pitt as you wait in a traffic jam, or Viggo Mortensen as you clean the house. Conjure up whoever turns you on and let your mind go where it will! This will help to give you a healthy glow and a twinkle in your eye! Read erotic fiction if this is something you enjoy, or, better still, write your own. As you interact with people, smile as if you share a sexy secret and make lots of eye contact with them.

Remind yourself daily that you are a smart, sexy, desirable woman. You are an exciting lover. You know your body better than anyone else on earth, and you know how to gain pleasure from it. You are flirtatious and exciting – any man would be lucky to spend time with you!

Here are a few simple tips to enhance your natural allure:

◆ Wear beautiful lingerie and night clothes.
◆ Treat yourself to an expensive, exotic perfume.
◆ Develop a sexy smile.
◆ Dance often.
◆ Wear red lipstick in a shade that suits your colouring.

You now have lots of ways to develop your radiance, mystery and allure. Work on these feminine qualities daily and incorporate them into your chosen persona. You will soon be feeling like a whole new woman, full of magnetic power!

Enchantress

My raven tresses are flowing loose
Over a velvet gown of wine.
My deep-red cloak is swirling round
As the moon in a mist does shine.
The powers of Circe dwell in me
As I weave and cast my spell.
The power of magic flows through me
By candle, book and bell.
With herb, leaf, bud and flower
Powders and potions I make.
I stir the cauldron, tap the wand
And scry in the sacred lake.
By Earth, Air, Water, Fire
And elementals I command;
I summon your heart's true desire
And see destiny in your hand.
Leafing through my sacred book,
Looking for the charm,
I can banish all your enemies
And prevent them doing harm.
I read my own fate in the stars,
And if I don't like what I see,
I cast a spell, make a change,
Create a new destiny.
I cast the sacred circle round;
I wear the crown of the crescent moon;
I call the quarters and state my need;
The Goddess always grants my boon.
High in my tower with cliff-top view
A magic mirror tells all to me.
To the Old Ways I am ever true;
An enchantress I will always be!

Morgana

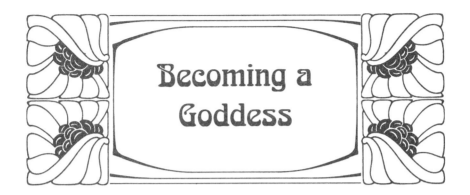

Becoming a Goddess

Throughout this book I have tried to illustrate the incredible force of goddess power that resides within every woman. True witchery is about being in tune with this power and using it to improve your life. In this chapter we will be looking at what it takes to live like a goddess!

Honour yourself

Goddesses come in many shapes and sizes. They are not all built like Aphrodite. This means that whatever your weight or shape you already have the body of a goddess. If you are active and healthy, it doesn't matter what your dress size is or how big your bum may be.

Your body does a hard job, day in and day out. It never takes time off. It is the vehicle that moves you through life, it is the medium through which your talents flow, it is the treasure chest holding the jewel of your spirit, and it has the potential to be the gateway of life for future generations. As such your body deserves your love and respect, for without it you'd be dead.

Treating your body as the sacred temple of your personal goddess spirit is a powerful way to change your attitude to your looks and physique. Your body is an amazing work of magic. It is self-healing, fighting off infections and healing wounds; it is nurturing, giving sustenance and comfort to its offspring; it is automatic, pumping blood and oxygen and processing fuel seemingly without effort. Your body is an incredible piece of construction. Honour it and be grateful for the gift of life it enables you to enjoy.

Regular exercise is one way to honour yourself, but this must be something you enjoy. If working out at the gym feels like a chore, do something else instead. Your exercise routine should bring you joy and happiness, so indulge in a sport or physical activity that brings you pleasure. Swimming, running, walking, taking part in a team sport, climbing, horse riding and so on, are all great ways to exercise and may well get you out and about too. You might also meet people with similar interests and strike up new friendships.

But perhaps the most goddess-inspired form of exercise is dance. Dancing can be exhilarating, fun, sexy, provocative, graceful or seductive. Whatever your abilities, there is some kind of dance out there that you could enjoy. Ballet is incredibly beautiful. It is disciplined and demanding and it strengthens the frame. Tap dancing and traditional Celtic dancing are fun and give you the chance to tap out any negative feelings; belly dancing is good for toning the hips and trimming down the waist; and if you want to try something really sexy, take a lap dancing class!

If you don't want to enrol in dance classes, just put on some music and dance away your stress at home. Dance has always been a part of a woman's sacred power. The ancient temple virgins would dance for their chosen gods and goddesses, so do indulge in this activity and use it to express yourself.

Pampering yourself occasionally will not only honour your body but will lift your spirits too. Visiting a spa and relaxing in a hot tub or having a massage will leave you feeling calm, rejuvenated and ready to take on the world. Having a manicure or a pedicure will increase your sense of personal beauty, while treatments such as reflexology and aromatherapy may relieve any ailments you are suffering from.

If money is scarce, you could turn your own bathroom into a spa by lighting candles and incense, playing soft New Age music and using a small bath spa to create the hot-tub effect. Give yourself a manicure, apply a face pack and a hair mask, and sip a cool glass of wine or spring water as you beautify yourself! All women should incorporate a beautician night into their weekly routine. This is a great way to feel good about yourself and keep your nails, hair and skin in tip-top condition. And you are a goddess, after all; you deserve to give yourself some quality time and attention!

Develop your own goddess style

Each goddess has her own style, charisma and flair. She has tokens and symbols that represent her and that express what she stands for. As you are a goddess in your own right, you need to take control of your image, and create your personal sense of style and chic. You could choose a style to enhance the persona you are creating for yourself, or you might prefer to experiment with various styles until you find one you like.

We could all take a tip from the world of fashion dolls, which seem to have a stunning outfit for every occasion. It's easy to pull on a pair of jeans and a sweater and run a comb through your hair without even thinking about it, but this doesn't honour your body and it certainly won't make you feel like a goddess. On the other hand, being a slave to fashion could leave you feeling like something of a clone, and will almost certainly put a large dent in your bank balance!

So how do you strike a balance between grabbing the first article of clothing you see and hitting your credit card limit for a pair of 'must have' designer shoes? The answer is, you create your own style, picking clothes that suit you and enhance your shape and colouring. In this way you will always look and feel great, without being a fashion victim or a hostage to your credit card. Decide what image you want for yourself, what kind of clothes would make you feel like a goddess, and furnish your wardrobe accordingly. This may take a little time, so don't worry if you can't get everything you want right away – changing your image won't happen overnight.

If you're short of cash, then be thrifty and remember the power of words: these days there is no such thing as 'hand me downs' and 'second-hand togs'; there is only the elegance of 'vintage'. Don't forget to think about accessories such as bags, purses, hair ornaments and footware. And think about your make-up style too. Does your look need an update? Or would you prefer a more natural make-up-free beauty image? Take your time and create the image of a goddess for yourself. Work your way through the following tips to develop a style that is chic, unique and all your own:

◆ Bring magic to your style by adding meaningful occult jewellery to your outfits.
◆ Create a basic colour palette of your choice and mix and match, remembering the principles of colour magic.
◆ Decide on a signature fabric, such as velvet, and wear it often.
◆ Decide on a signature designer perfume and treat yourself to a bottle.
◆ Incorporate your trademark token (for example, the butterfly) into your new style.

Creating a goddess book

Creating your own goddess book can also help you to develop your style. Use a hard-bound book and glue into it any pictures of clothes, jewellery, accessories, outfits and so on that you would like. This will give you a clear idea of what kind of image your inner goddess needs, as pictures speak directly to our subconscious. It will also serve to magnetise such items towards you, particularly if you look at the book often.

Raid fashion catalogues and magazines and cut out pictures of anything that would enhance your personal goddess style. Try hair magazines too, cutting out various styles and shades. This may inspire you to visit a salon for a restyle, or to grow your hair long. Don't forget the world of celebrities either. By no means should you try to become a carbon copy of a celebrity, as you are working to develop your own style here, but studying photos of glamorous famous people is a great way to get fashion tips. Celebrities often employ make-up artists, so make use of their expertise by copying your favourite celebrity's look. Choose someone whose hair and eye colour closely match your own for the best results. Do the same with hair styles and accessories. Make sure you are simply adding little bits and pieces to your own style, rather than copying a single celebrity look. The trick is to mix and match, taking the odd inspirational tip here and there, and mixing them into your own personal goddess style.

Look at your goddess book as often as you can, and continue to add to it over time, developing your style as you go.

Creating your temple

All goddesses have temples dedicated to them, and you should be no exception to this rule! Your home is your temple, so begin to see it in this way. Of course, some rooms are more temple-like than others – the bedroom, for example, with its atmosphere of peace, love and calm, is a temple in its own right. But your entire home should be a temple dedicated to you and your inner goddess. Think

back to the seven female icons: your home is your castle and you are the queen of your own realm. These are very empowering thoughts. If you begin to view your home in this sacred way, you will feel quite differently about it, and in turn about yourself.

Turn your home into a sacred temple by burning candles, fragrant oils and incenses, and filling it with fresh flowers. Play relaxing New Age music and place pictures and statues of goddesses all around. When you next have time off from work or the children, treat yourself to a 'temple day'. Relax, work magic, and honour yourself and your inner goddess. Sip a glass of wine, burn your favourite oils, light the room with candles and relax.

You might even want to create a temple robe for yourself for such occasions. This should be long, loose and comfortable, so think about buying a velvet dress, a Grecian-style night dress, or some kind of kaftan. Alternatively, you could buy a custom-made Wiccan robe from an occult shop or wear your witch's cloak as a robe instead. If you have skill with a sewing machine, you could design and create your own temple robe, embroidering it with your initials, magical name or a personal trademark symbol. Let your imagination go and have a little fun!

If you've always loved the Medieval gowns of Camelot and Middle Earth, treat yourself to one and wear it around the house as your temple robe. This is your home, after all, and you can wear whatever you like, so treat your inner goddess to an extra special outfit. If you are interested in the sacred aspects of home-making read my book *How to Create a Magical Home.*

Sacred creativity

Women are naturally creative. We cook, paint, sew, write, tend the garden, have babies and so on. The urge to create something new is innate in most women, but some of us have lost touch with our creativity and are so wrapped up in getting through the day that we never think to make time for our creative talents.

Everybody has a creative talent of some kind. You may already know what your talent is or you may need to rediscover it. Thinking back to your school days may help you to get back in touch with your creativity. Which classes did you particularly like? Did you enjoy English literature or music lessons? Maybe you loved art or drama. What you enjoyed in school and had a natural aptitude for may be where your creative talents lie. On the other hand, if creative subjects were very academically taught at your school, they may have stemmed the flow of creative juices, putting you off something that you once loved. For instance, I love reading and writing poetry, but I hated having to analyse it stanza by stanza for my degree course. It was only when I'd finished studying and could enjoy poetry in my own way that I willingly picked up an anthology again.

Sit for a moment and remember what you enjoyed doing when you were a child. Then decide to make time for this in your life. Most of us have more than one creative talent to tap into. You may enjoy writing, dancing and needlework, for example (but hate cookery and art). Wherever your particular talents lie, make time to get back in tune with them, for they are a gift from the powers that be and could even turn out to be your life's work. Lots of people make an extremely good living doing exactly what they love to do. Pop stars, film actors, celebrity chefs and bestselling authors all have one thing in common: they tapped into their talents, were true to their goals and made a great deal of money out of them.

Whatever your talent may be, dedicate yourself to it and see where it takes you. You've been given your talent for a reason, so don't neglect it. Do something today that will put you back in touch with it. This could mean digging out an old musical instrument, signing up for salsa classes, or buying new art supplies, needlework equipment or equestrian gear. If you like to sing, invest in a home karaoke system and make your own demo tapes, or simply put on your favourite CD and belt out a number. Do something today that will bring out your sacred gift of creativity and enjoy your goddess-given talent.

The ring of power

The ring is a symbol of eternity, because it has no end and no beginning. It is also a representation of the sacred magic circle. Many witches choose to wear a special ring to symbolise their path and their dedication to the Craft. These rings come in various styles, such as a pentacle, triquetra, spiral and Celtic  knotwork, but generally all are made of silver, as this is the metal of the Goddess.

Your Craft ring should be worn on your third finger (the one next to your little finger) to demonstrate that you have a special commitment to your magical path. If you are single, you might like to wear your ring on your left hand in a form of independent self-declaration. This tradition was started by Queen Elizabeth I, who refused all marriage proposals and took to wearing her ring of sovereignty on her wedding finger, allegedly stating, 'I am married to England'. Now there's a declaration of independence for you! This is an empowering practice, but not one to be taken lightly, as you will be dedicating yourself to the Craft and the Old Ways.

Choose your ring of power with care. It should be of a design that makes you think of witchcraft and the power of magic, yet it should also represent who you are and fit in with your personal style and persona. A ring that incorporates a crystal such as a moonstone or your birth stone would be ideal, as would a ring of Celtic knotwork if you have Celtic blood, or a ring designed to fit in with your chosen persona – for example, one fashioned to look like a snowflake would be ideal if you have taken on the ice maiden persona.

Dedicating your ring

Once you have your ring, dedicate it to yourself and your Craft in the following way.

◆ Leave the ring on your pentacle in the light of the full moon to charge. While it is charging, write a few words to express how you feel about dedicating yourself to the Old Ways via this special token.

◆ The following evening, have a relaxing bath and put on your temple robe if you have one, or a comfortable night dress.

◆ Go to your altar, light the candles and speak the words you have written.

◆ Pick up the ring and place it on your third finger. Say:

I am dedicated to my Craft as a witch.
This ring is a symbol of my power.
Blessed be!

◆ Sit for a while in meditation, then snuff out the candles and go about your evening.

You now wear a ring of power and a sign of your Craft. It will remind you every day to be true to yourself, to strive towards your goals and to live up to the title of witch. Most importantly, it will remind you that you are a goddess in your own right. Blessed be!

Ice Maiden

She stands alone on a moonlit night,
Immune as the frost begins to bite.
Her heart is cold, she feels no chill,
This feisty maiden with an iron will.
Her stare can turn your blood to ice
And chill your bones in a trice.
Her skin is soft and white as snow,
But hoar frost forms where tears should flow.
Her freezing touch invokes a gasp.
She is numbed by pain from winters past.
Strong as the snow-capped mountains white,
Frozen in time when love took flight,
Hiding behind an ice-cool mask,
Freezing out those who take her to task,
Concealing her wounds behind a glacial wall,
She keeps her fragility hidden from all.
With tools of the Arctic she builds her defence
And shuts people out with a wintry fence.
From love's harsh blows her frailty sheltered ...
Yet the wish of her heart is but to be melted.

Morgana

Get a Life!

Witches take control of their lives. We know that personal responsibility is the key to success, and we take full responsibility for the realisation of our own goals and ambitions. Many people drift through life, floating from day to day with no clear goal to work towards. But somewhere inside we all have dreams, however unambitious we may believe ourselves to be.

I believe that anyone with a sincere interest in witchcraft is looking for a way to change some aspect of their lives. You may wish to become more spiritual, or more empowered, or more attuned with nature, or any one of a wide range of things, but if you've picked up this book and read this far, you are probably looking to make a few life improvements.

And you've come to the right place. Any aspect of your life can be improved using witchcraft. Health, finances, love life, family relationships, career prospects, creativity ... all can be improved with the right tools and the right frame of mind. We have already looked at the basic components of a successful spell. In this chapter we will be looking at the components of a successful life. All magic must be backed up in a mundane way in order to be effective. Here we will be exploring various techniques and strategies to make sure you get the best results possible from your magic and from your life in general.

It can be very disheartening when spells have little or no effect. In this chapter we will be looking at key practical ways in which you can make sure this does not happen. I want your spells to be successful. I want you to become an adept and competent witch. The last thing I want is for your spells to fail because you were in the wrong frame of mind, or you didn't have a clear goal, or you failed to back them up properly. I want you to be successful in all that you do, so that you can live a happy and fulfilled life as an empowered wise woman and witch.

So let's take a look at how you can use your power in the everyday world to influence the universal energies around you to bring you what you need. In short, you are going to learn how to design your life so that it fits you perfectly. It's time to stop drifting and start taking charge of your destiny!

The power of positive thinking

Witches are well aware of the power of thought. We are what we think, and what we focus on the most is exactly what we pull into our lives. We are self-fulfilling prophecies. If you are interested in sport, you will probably have come across the phrase 'positive mental attitude', or PMA for short. This technique is at the very core of all success stories. Maintaining a positive attitude is crucial if you want to realise your ambitions and live the life of your dreams.

And your dreams really can come true! The reason we have so-called 'pipe dreams' is so that we can catch a glimpse of our true potential. Our dreams show us what we could be, what we could achieve for ourselves if only we had the courage to try and the determination to just keep trying until we succeeded.

Most of us have suffered from negative programming over the years without our even being aware of it. People may have told you that dreaming is a waste of time, that you'll never make anything of your life, that the best you can possibly hope for is 'just enough to get by'. These people may even have tried to make you feel guilty for wanting more and for not being content to settle for what you have. Negative people will trudge off to work day after day, to a job that they dislike, and then spend their lives complaining about it instead of doing something to change it. Such people may take a negative interest in your goals and ambitions, asking if you've accomplished them yet – but this is usually only so that they can smile smugly when you admit that, no, you're not quite where you'd like to be just yet. I'm sure you all know someone like this, for this type of person is unfortunately very common. Wouldn't you love to wipe that smug smile off their face once and for all by proving them wrong and achieving every single goal you make for yourself? Well, now – with the help of this chapter – you can!

As a magical enchantress and powerful witch, you know that simply wishing is not enough to make your dreams come true. You know all that goes into a successful spell and you can apply this knowledge to your life. This is the real secret behind success and the 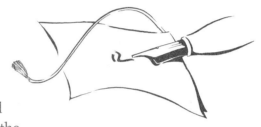 manifestation of your dreams. It takes a lot more than a wish list to make your dreams come true; it takes belief in yourself and your goal, a positive attitude, determination, and the courage to go against the flow and pull against the tide of the masses.

It takes a certain amount of resilience, too, to hold fast to your dream in the face of scepticism and scorn. You may be accused of selfishness, laziness, pipe dreaming, delusions of grandeur, unreliability and any number of other things. But all that really matters is that you are true to yourself and to your goal. The bottom line is that it is the most negative people who are usually the most dissatisfied with their own lives. They are simply envious of anyone who has the courage to try something different or attempt to better themselves in some way. Don't let these people make you feel bad for wanting something more for yourself. Just remember that positive thinking has power and you are a self-fulfilling prophecy. What you imagine yourself to be, you will become. Smile to yourself in the knowledge that your success will bring its own rewards.

Take control of your goals starting today. Begin a new life for yourself right now by committing to the fulfilment of your dreams. Refuse to be influenced by those who tell you that 'you should be so lucky'. Simply smile and say, 'Yes, I am.' Strive to create a beautiful and successful reality for yourself. Don't let any negativity get in your way. Don't give up before a long list of reasons why you can't achieve your goal. These are just excuses, created by the negative collective unconscious to make you think that you cannot succeed. Remember that you are a powerful woman and a witch. Biologically speaking, you have the potential to create a whole new life inside you, so surely you can manage to achieve a few goals!

The art of being selfish

Is selfishness a bad thing? We are conditioned to believe so. But in order to be truly commited to your goals you will have to act a little selfishly. I believe, however, that the world would be a much happier place if we were all a little more selfish.

The kind of selfishness I am talking about is following our own life path and doing that which serves us best. Many people are a hostage to the needs of others – parents, partners, children and so on. While it is commendable to care about others, we all have to learn to draw the line and take time to move our own life forward. I'm not advocating that you totally disregard the needs of others, but what I am saying is that your life is precious, your time is precious, so don't give it all away to other people. Keep some for yourself and for the pursuit of your personal dreams and ambitions. If you allow yourself to fall into a rut, your life will stagnate. Try to make sure your life is constantly progressing at a steady pace and in the direction you most want to go. In following your own life path you will be more fulfilled and far less stressed. You will be happier in general, and your happiness will spread, making other people happy too.

Doing nothing at all can sometimes make us feel guilty, but I feel it is as important to have some days of relaxation and meditation as it is to have days of activity. Just sitting in contemplation of where your life is going can give your brain the time it needs to inspire you with a fabulous idea. This idea may be related to your career, or to your home, or to how you can move your life towards your ultimate goal. If you are constantly on the go, you may be missing out on a vital source of inspiration from your higher self. So be selfish enough to take a little time out. Read a book, watch a film, day-dream, take a nap or simply be. No shame, no guilt, no excuses. Just sit for a while and enjoy doing ... well, not very much at all!

Discovering your life's work

In the last chapter we looked at developing your creative talents. In this section we will be delving a little deeper and discovering your life's work. Witches believe that there

is a reason for everything, which means that there is a reason for you! You are here for a purpose. You have been blessed with a unique set of talents, gifts and personality traits, all of which will be of use to you in your life's work.

You are more than a face in a crowd, more than just a member of the work force, more than a simple statistic. Of course, you already know all of this, but it doesn't hurt to have it acknowledged once in a while, does it? My point is that you are unique, and you have a unique role in life. It may be the role you are playing now or it may be one you are not yet filling, but whatever it is, it will bring you abundance, recognition and happiness. Discovering your life's role is the key to becoming successful. Once you know what path you are naturally drawn to, it becomes easier to work towards it and manifest your dreams.

Creative talents are a clue as to where your life's work may be. For example, I have wanted to be writer ever since I was a child. I was constantly scribbling stories and poems. I have always been a bookworm, and my favourite subject in school was English. After leaving school, I worked steadily towards my goal, and as a result I am now a full-time author, making my living doing what I love to do.

Your own creative talents may be a part of your current job or career, or they may be completely separate. But you should be aware that they could form the basis of your life's work. If you have always harboured a secret dream to be an artist, dancer, musician, nurse, detective or writer, then listen to what your dreams are telling you, for this could be your true path in life. Whatever you love to do, this is where your life's work can be found, and you can craft yourself a successful career doing exactly what you love to do.

Most successful entrepreneurs began their life's work by tapping into a personal talent, interest or hobby. They put their heart into their work and, because they loved what they were doing, they gave it their all. Eventually their effort paid off, sometimes yielding huge financial dividends. Take Richard Branson, for example. He was a teenager with a love of pop music. On the basis of that love he has built his own empire and made himself a fortune.

Unless you take the first step, you will never know where the road could lead. There are no limits to what you can achieve other than those you impose upon yourself, so take a moment right now to think about what you would be doing with your life if you could do absolutely anything. The answer to that question is likely to be the key to your life's work and the purpose of your unique talents and gifts. Don't allow doubt and fear to hold you back. Just take a deep breath and go for it!

Create a life plan

We have said that witches tend not to drift through life. We usually have a very clear idea of where we are going and where we want to be in ten years' time. We use magic and witchcraft to help us get there, but we also use something a little more mundane. In order to arrive at your destination, it is vital that you create some kind of life plan for yourself, for unless you have a map to your destiny, how are you going to reach it?

It may seem obvious that knowing where you want your life to go is crucial to any degree of success, but it is surprising how many people focus more on what they don't want than on what they do! And, as you now know, what you focus on is exactly what you get, so this kind of negative thought pattern is the equivalent to shooting yourself in the foot.

In this section of the book, therefore, you are going to make a few important decisions about what you really want from life – how you want your personal reality to be. You will need a pad and a pen and some quiet time alone.

Before you begin, ask yourself this empowering question:

If I could have and do ANYTHING,
what would my life be like?

Try not to put any limitations on your answer. Just speak from the soul, allowing your deepest dreams and ambitions to arise. Once you have some idea of the answer, you have a general image of your ideal life. Now begin to describe it in detail. Remember, you can have anything you want.

In all likelihood there will be something of a gap between where you are now and where you want to be. To bridge that gap, make a list of all the steps you need to take to move towards your ideal life. This will give you a rough plan of your chosen road and how far you have to go. You now have a blueprint to work from. Taking one step at a time, you will eventually be living the life of your dreams. In the meantime, set a few goals to improve your current lifestyle by working through the sections below. Write out your goals for each of the following areas so that you have a clear representation of where your life is heading in every arena.

Relationships

Don't allow any of your relationships to fall into a rut. Work on your communications with people. Keep in touch and don't let any relationship become one-sided – make the effort! Friends, family and lovers are all equally important. Cherish them and nurture the circle of love that surrounds you. At the same time, know when a relationship has run its course and it is time to call it a day. Decide on one action you will take regularly to improve and enhance your relationships. Be specific and make your action manageable.

Finances

Make some plans to improve your current finances. This could mean working over-time, becoming self-employed, changing from part-time to full-time employment or cutting back on non-essential spending. If you are in debt, make a pay-back plan and stick to it. Throw away catalogues and cut up credit cards. Open a savings account and set up standing orders to pay all your household bills. Take full control of your finances – don't allow your finances to control you!

Career

If you have a career, decide where you want it to go. If, on the other hand, you work sporadically in minimum-wage employment, consider whether you would like a career or profession. If you don't like your current job, change it and try something different. If you seem to be forever drifting from one dead-end job to another, make an effort to discover your life's work and set about creating a career for yourself that you will truly love. Go to college or night school. Sign up with the Open University. Start your own business. You don't have to spend your life in a job you don't like. There are thousands of options and opportunities out there – the first step to achieving something is to pick one!

Body image

Very few people are completely happy with their body image. Before you decide that you need to make changes to yours, you should re-read Chapter 10 and be sure to honour yourself! However, there is nothing wrong with taking steps to improve the way you look. If you need to lose weight, start on a sensible weight-loss plan. If you're too thin, make an effort to eat adequately. Start doing regular exercise if you don't already, get a new hair cut, have a facial or a manicure. Make your improvements to the way you look part of loving and revering yourself.

Leisure

Carve out a little space for yourself in your busy life. Take up a new hobby – or an old one. Learn a new skill. Improve your mind with extensive reading, expand your vocabulary or try learning a new language. Remember to make plenty of time for your magic and witchcraft. Set yourself the task of learning a particular branch of the Craft, such as herbalism or Tarot reading. Just enjoy being you for a while!

Once you have worked your way through the above sections and made your notes, you will have a complete life plan that takes care of the present and the future. Follow this plan to help you achieve your dreams. Add a little spellcraft and witchery, and your goals will soon be well on the way to being realised.

Black Hats and Broomsticks

Tall black hats and broomsticks,
The symbols of the witch's trade.
In perfect love and perfect trust,
With harm to none our spells are made.

If you hear a voice at night
Calling you in dreams,
If you feel the magic
Of the silver moonlight beams,

If you dance at midnight
And raise your voice in song,
If you come across a magic ring,
Then you're back where you belong.

You may call upon the Goddess;
She always knows her own,
For you've been on this path before,
And the Goddess calls you home.

Morgana

Black Hats
and Broomsticks

So far we have looked at the various components of witchcraft and self-empowerment. But what does being a witch in today's world really mean? Well, as we have seen, it certainly won't make life a total breeze! Being a dedicated witch is a continuous learning curve; it entails a lot of hard work and is very time-consuming. It also entails accepting that bad things sometimes happen to good people. We can cast spells to ease pain or to strengthen courage, but we cannot cast an effective spell for a completely trouble-free existence. In any case, without the rain we wouldn't appreciate the sunshine, and without the lows we cannot fully experience the highs.

Being a witch means being a wise woman, and part of that is knowing when the wisest action to take is simply to do nothing. It is knowing when to speak out and when to remain silent; when to rally to a cause and when to take a step back; when to fight and when to retreat so that you may fight from a stronger position on another day.

Being a witch means taking full personal responsibility for your life in word, thought and deed – even when others around you prefer to blame someone or something else. Being a witch means being strong enough to admit when you're wrong, clever enough to admit when you don't understand, tough enough to ask for help when you need it, and smart enough to learn from those who are more knowledgeable than you. It means absorbing the lessons of life and taking the hard knocks on the chin. It is knowing that the secret to taking life in your stride is to constantly readjust your step.

Witchcraft is about being true to yourself and working to improve yourself and your circumstances. It means being controlled enough to keep your temper and act with dignity, and it means helping and supporting those weaker than yourself, spreading positivity and guiding them to their own source of empowerment. It is knowing when to cut ties with any negative person or influence on your life. It is overcoming bad habits and generally trying on a daily basis to be all that you can be. It is about having complete faith in yourself and in the universal energies of love and abundance. It's a tall order, isn't it? But I never said that witchcraft was easy!

Coming out of the broom closet

The word 'witch' is a title, and like most titles it carries not only a weight of responsibility but also a set of preconceived associations. I was recently dubbed 'the official witch of England'. While I was flattered and honoured to have been given such an accolade, I was also a little embarrassed, as there are many witches throughout the UK who all work hard to dispel the myths of the stereotypical witch. Hopefully, you will become one of them.

When you call yourself a witch, you are setting yourself apart from the crowd, and this may mean that you become something of a focal point for other people. It can also lead to you being misunderstood and even feared, especially by people whose only concept of a witch is the evil-doing old hag. Once you have decided that witchcraft is the right path for you, you will probably want to tell your family and close friends about your new interest – if only to explain why you're never available on the night of the full moon! Give them this book to read so that they fully understand the path you have chosen and the positive, empowering reasons for taking it. They may still be slightly bemused, but once they see how much more balanced and fulfilled you are as a woman in your own right, they will probably accept your decision, because they know you well, love you and trust your judgement.

However, don't blurt out your new magical identity to just anyone. Unfortunately, prejudice is still a part of society, and however much you explain about the positivity and gentleness of the Craft, there will always be those narrow-minded individuals who insist that witchcraft is evil. Take care who you tell in your place of work. Don't put your career in the spotlight for the wrong reasons!

By the same token, though, you shouldn't go out of your way to hide your spirituality and dedication to the Old Ways, as this could be counter-productive. Once people get to know you as a kind and helpful person, they will probably come to think that maybe witchcraft is a good thing after all. And to more perceptive people your magic will simply shine through.

If you wear a pentacle necklace or other occult jewellery, expect to be questioned about it. If you're not happy declaring yourself as a witch, then simply say that you are interested in 'alternative therapies and spiritualities' or that you are studying 'women's mysteries and the non-political feminist movement'. All of this is true. You have simply left out the title 'witch'. Use your judgement. Come out of the broom closet in your own time and make sure you can explain the Craft clearly and simply, because you will almost certainly be put on the spot!

To take on the title of witch is to shoulder the responsibility for demonstrating that the Craft is a positive, empowering and gentle practice that harms none. It means doing your bit to reverse the disservice the Burning Times did for witches and womankind. It means supporting and standing shoulder to shoulder with your sister witches as we try to bring about the widespread unconditional acceptance of the Craft – and it means never doing or saying anything that brings the Old Ways into disgrace.

If you choose to call yourself a witch, you must live up to some very high expectations. It is not a title to be taken lightly, so make sure you are adopting it for the right reasons.

Lead, don't follow

Witches are empowered women who have a strong sense of their own individuality. As such they tend to be natural leaders. My motto has always been 'Lead, don't follow'. Why be a sheep in the flock when you can be a wolf and go your own way? In general, true witches tend not to follow the crowd. They don't jump on any bandwagon that happens to be passing. This means that they will only watch the World Cup if they have a passionate interest in football! They are not slaves to fashion and they have their own unique style. If straight hair is the thing, a witch is likely to invest in a set of curling tongs! We don't conform.

Take a good look at yourself and your life. Do you follow the masses? Do you leap on the bandwagon for fear of being left behind? If so, don't! There will always be another one along in a minute! Don't waste your life leaping from one to the next.

Affirm to yourself that from now on you will lead not follow, that you will start trends not follow them slavishly. Look to yourself for guidance and inspiration, not to the crowd.

When life gets in the way

In general, witchcraft and daily life go hand in hand, enhancing and complementing one another to add up to a rich, empowered and fulfilled life. There will be occasions, however, when witchcraft may have to be put on the back burner for a while because it could be detrimental to work magic and ritual at this time. For example, if you are going through an illness or have suffered a bereavement, all your energies will be needed for your recovery. If you are busy taking care of a sick relative, you may not have the time, energy and focus left to cast an effective spell, so it is better to wait a little while until you can give the spell your full attention. In such cases it is permissible to take time out from the Craft for a few days or weeks.

There is one thing that is notorious for getting in the way of witchcraft, and that's men! In days of old, the village witch or wise woman would generally remain unmarried and would live alone. There is a sound reason for this – it meant that she could devote herself to the Craft without having the complication of a man making demands on her time.

Although men are generally fascinated by the idea of witchcraft, they may not like it when it absorbs a lot of their partner's time. Finding a balance between your witchcraft and your relationship can be difficult, but it's not impossible. It is much easier if your partner is of a magical mind or is himself Wiccan. This way you will both understand the importance of the Craft and can work rituals together. But if this is not the case, you must stand your ground and insist that you have time and space to practise your Craft. Try suggesting that he go out with the lads when you are working rituals. You will then have the house to yourself and you will also know that your partner is enjoying himself with his friends.

If you live apart from your partner, make sure you keep a few nights free for your magic, especially around the time of the full moon. Try not to schedule dates on this night and don't fall into the trap of spending all evening talking to him on the phone. Be independent, mysterious and just get on with your life as a witch. If you allow your partner to take up all your time and don't make a stand, you may come to resent him and feel that you are missing something in your life.

If I have to take time out from witchcraft, I feel a sense of loss and an emptiness inside. The Craft is such a huge part of my life and daily existence that if I haven't spent time at my altar or worked any magic for a while, I begin to feel like a shadow of myself. As soon as I spend a day doing witchy things such as reading or writing Craft books, working on my Book of Shadows and working magic at my altar, I feel whole again. I am recharged and ready to take on the challenges of life. I am happier in myself and therefore better company for family and friends.

So if you do need to take time away from your witchcraft, don't be surprised when you miss it. You are a witch and the magic flows through you constantly, whether you use it or not. Honour your power by blending witchcraft into your life and make time to reconnect with your magic on a regular basis.

Witch's Song

Hear now the witch's song.
Days grow dark and nights are long.
See autumn mists go swirling by,
Hear the barn owl's screeching cry
Calling witches out to play
While husbands fast asleep still lie!

They gather in the woods at night
All aglow with camp fire light.
Round about the flames they dance,
Twisting, turning, lost in trance.
Faster, faster, round they go,
Drawing power from the earth below.

Thirteen voices speak the charm
To keep their coven safe from harm.
The spell is cast, their work complete
Until once again they merry meet!
Then fast away on broomstick flight,
Gliding through the dead of night.

A smile plays upon her lips
As through the silent house she slips.
Her husband, filled with sleeping charms,
Rolls and takes her in his arms
Never knowing that his wife
Enjoys a secret witch's life!

Morgana

Your Spell Collection

No book on magic would be complete without a few spells! However, it is important to say that each witch should begin to write her own spells as soon as possible, as they will then be personal to her and her circumstances. The spells you write yourself will always be more powerful than the ones you use from books, because they come from within you and are a product of your personal goddess power. Writing your first rituals however, can be a bit daunting, so this chapter contains a few of my favourite spells to get you started on your magical path. Use them as blueprints for when you create your own rituals, drawing on the information in this book as a foundation and a guideline. Before you start, here are a few tips to ensure your success in different types of spell-casting.

Tips for spells of love and passion

Never cast these spells with a particular person in mind. This is known as bending another person's will and goes against the Wiccan Rede (see page 20). Instead, always cast love spells around your ideal of a lover. Try to be as specific as possible. If all you want is friendship, state this in your spell. If you're after a fling or even just a bootie call, own up to it and say that this is what you want. True love may take a while to manifest, and it won't come knocking on your door, so when you've performed your spell, get out and meet new people to back it up.

Tips for spells of wealth and prosperity

Only ask for what you need plus a little more and learn to view money as energy. It can never truly be taken away or lost to you; it only changes shape and form. Trust in the natural abundance of the universe and know that you will always be provided for in some way. You should cast all spells with harm to none, and this is particularly important when it comes to money spells. Money can come from negative sources such as insurance after a death or compensation for an accident, so make sure your wealth is increased in a positive manner, keeping the Wiccan Rede in mind at all times (see page 20). Finally, remember the Threefold Law (see page 21) and give to charity. Not only will you be helping someone else but your finances will be replenished threefold!

Tips for spells of power and protection

With this type of magic the emphasis is on prevention rather than cure. Protection spells are usually meant to be worked on a regular basis to weave a magical web of armour around yourself and your home. Spells to increase power and to recharge magical tools should be worked at the time of the full moon for best results.

Use these tips to enhance and empower all your spell-castings and to create the kind of life you want for yourself. Remember to back up all your spells in the everyday world with positive actions. Happy spell-casting!

Lucky leaves prosperity spell

Purpose of spell: to attract money to your purse

What you need: 3 dried bay leaves, patchouli essential oil, a paint brush, your purse

Moon phase: waxing

- ◆ Take all the items to your altar.
- ◆ Using the paintbrush, dab each of the leaves with the oil and leave them to dry.
- ◆ When the leaves are dry, place them in your purse to magically draw money towards you.

Spell to magnetise abundance

Purpose of spell: to bring abundance and prosperity into your life

What you need: a white candle and a suitable holder, a green pen, a lodestone (a type of magnet, available from New Age and occult stores)

Moon phase: waxing

◆ Sit before your altar. Make sure you are comfortable.

◆ Hold the unlit candle for a while, concentrating on the gifts of abundance.

◆ Take the green pen and write 'abundance' on one palm and 'prosperity' on the other. Don't worry about any money troubles you may have – keep your thoughts positive.

◆ Place the lodestone before the candle and light the wick.

◆ Position your hands on either side of the candle, with your palms open and upwards. Close your eyes and visualise unlimited abundance flowing into your hands. Repeat the following charm, continuing for as long as you are focused and comfortable:

I magnetise prosperity and abundance.

◆ Let the candle burn out and go about your day.

Spell to find love

Purpose of spell: to bring a lover into your life
What you need: a red candle and a suitable holder, your favourite essential oil, a pen, a piece of paper
Moon phase: full

◆ Working at your altar, anoint the red candle with the essential oil.
◆ Write a list of all that you want in a lover and companion, then fold the list carefully.
◆ Light the candle and speak the following charm three times:

> *With these words this spell I sow.*
> *Bring the love I've yet to know.*
> *Fill my heart and set it aglow,*
> *Secrets only witches know.*
> *I take the power and let it go!*
> *As I will, it shall be so!*

◆ Burn the spell paper and wait for your love to come to you.

Queen of Hearts spell

Be warned, if you don't like to be the centre of attention or would feel hounded if pursued, this spell is not for you!

Purpose of spell: to become popular with men
What you need: a red candle and a suitable holder, the Queen of Hearts card, a pen
Moon phase: waxing

◆ Write your name in all four corners of the Queen of Hearts card. This will ensure your ability to attract from all directions.
◆ Place the card face up and focus on it as you hold the unlit red candle. Concentrate on being attractive and desirable. Visualise yourself surrounded by adoring suitors – you are the temptress personified!
◆ Put the candle in the holder and place this on top of the card. Light the wick and allow the candle to burn down to release the magic you have created.

Angelic protection spell

Purpose of spell: to call your guardian angel
What you need: a white candle and a suitable holder
Moon phase: any – the angels are always available!

◆ Light the candle, close your eyes and visualise your guardian angel. Call to this being in the following way:

> *Guardian angel, bring your light;*
> *Make my future days as bright.*
> *Bring with you an angelic shield,*
> *As your mighty sword you wield.*
> *Embrace me with protective wings;*
> *Guard me from all harmful things.*
> *I call you here your power to lend,*
> *And welcome the love of an angel friend.*
> *So mote it be!*

◆ Allow the candle to burn down and know that you are protected by angels.

Spell to make a red witch love potion

This alcoholic potion has quite a kick, so make sure you choose a time to do this spell when you don't have to drive anywhere.

Purpose of spell: to draw in new love
Moon phase: waxing to full
What you need: a 300 ml/½ pint glass, a bottle of cider, a shot of pernod, some blackcurrant cordial, a cinnamon stick, a cocktail cherry, cherry plum Bach flower remedy

- Pour the shot of pernod into the glass and then fill it almost to the top with cider.
- Add enough blackcurrant cordial to turn the drink a deep red.
- Add three drops of cherry plum Bach flower remedy.
- Place the cocktail cherry on the end of the cinnamon stick and put it into the glass, cherry end down.
- Use the stick to stir the potion nine times deosil (clockwise), as you do so chanting continuously:

> *By Venus and Pan,*
> *I summon a Man!*

- Drink the potion while visualising your ideal partner.

Spell to call a familiar

Lots of witches choose to share their lives and their homes with an animal companion. These companions are known in magic as familiars – and they are much, much more than everyday pets. A familiar will usually come to you out of the blue. It may be a stray who adopts you or it may be brought to you by a friend or family member as a rescue animal in need of a good home. Your familiar will have a very close relationship with you, probably sharing with you a psychic bond. For instance, you may communicate wordlessly with your familar in dreams. Familiars are generally fascinated by magic and will watch you as you cast spells, perform divinations and so on.

My own familiar is a big black cat called Pyewackett, who came to me about six months after I performed a similar spell to this one. However, familiars don't have to be feline. Dogs, rats, snakes, hamsters, rabbits and even horses all make excellent familiars and companions in magic. You just need to trust that the right familiar will come to you at the right time.

If the idea of working magically with animals and familiars appeals to you, check out my book *Magical Beasts*.

Purpose of spell: to call a pet and familiar into your life
What you need: a pen and a slip of paper
Moon phase: full

◆ On the slip of paper write down a description of the kind of pet you want – cat, dog, horse, etc. Then think about colour, gender, temperament and any other characteristics that are important and write these down too.

◆ Build up a picture of your familiar in your mind's eye and focus on him, silently telling him that you will give him a safe and pleasant home, good food, and lots of love and care through health, sickness and old age.

◆ Bury the slip of paper in your garden or in a potted plant, still holding the image of your familiar in your mind. Now repeat the following charm three times:

> *I send these words on the spirit winds*
> *A magical familiar here to bring,*
> *One of loyalty and temperament sweet;*
> *By powers of telepathy our minds will meet.*
> *Magical, affectionate, faithful and true,*
> *Powerful familiar I now call you.*
> *Come to me by land or sea;*
> *Come to me I summon thee.*
> *Come to me by earth, by air;*
> *Come to me my home to share.*
> *Come to me; do not hide;*
> *I summon thee to my side.*
> *So mote it be!*

Spell to help a troubled family

Sometimes it can seem as if a dark cloud is hanging over your family. Trouble plagues you wherever you go. Bad luck, ill health, poverty and so on can create a sense of helplessness and hopelessness, leaving you feeling as if nothing good ever happens to you or your loved ones. But there is a simple magical answer. Dragon's blood incense is used by witches to clear away negative energy. Try this spell to blow away the dark clouds that have been shadowing you. You should soon see an improvement in your family's circumstances.

Purpose of spell: to ease the situation when your family is going through a difficult time
What you need: dragon's blood incense (available from occult stores)
Moon phase: any – perform daily for three weeks

◆ Go to your altar and light a stick of the incense. As it burns, focus on the positive things in your family life.

◆ Continue to light a stick of incense and meditate on the good things in your family life every day for the next three weeks. This will free up your universal space, allowing room for good things to come into it.

Spell to make a healing pouch

Purpose of spell: to make a healing bag for one who is sick
What you need: an acorn, a dried flower, a dried leaf, a quartz crystal, an amethyst crystal, an angel pin or other small angel figure (available from New Age stores), a pearl bead, a silver pentacle necklace, a fairy pin or other small fairy figure (available from New Age stores), a white feather, a butterfly charm, a love heart charm, a blue pouch, lavender oil, your pentacle, blue paper, a blue pen
Moon phase: full

◆ On the night of the full moon, place the acorn, flower, leaf, crystals, angel pin, bead, pentacle necklace, fairy pin, feather, butterfly charm and love heart charm on your pentacle to charge overnight.

◆ Write out the following spell on the blue paper using the blue pen.

> An acorn for strength when times are tough,
> A flower for friendship when life gets rough,
> A leaf for renewal, a seashell for healing,
> A clear quartz crystal to bestow good feeling,
> An amethyst crystal to bring peace and love,
> An angel to protect with powers from above,
> An ocean pearl to help ease the tears,
> A magical star to calm the fears,
> A fairy to help you rise above,
> A feather to invoke the peace of the dove,
> A butterfly token as a positive sign,
> A heart to prove you'll always have mine:
> These tokens of spellcraft I give to thee
> To heal and protect. Blessed be!

◆ Place the spell paper on the pentacle with the other items.
◆ The following morning, place all the tokens in the pouch, then fold the spell paper and add this too.
◆ Sprinkle the pouch with a few drops of the lavender oil and then give it to the person you seek to heal, with a wish for speedy recovery.

A spell for general happiness

Purpose of spell: to increase your sense of happiness and general well-being.
What you need: a tea-light, a tea-light-holder
Moon phase: any – perform daily

◆ Light the tea-light and place it in the holder.
◆ Hold your hands out to either side of the flame and repeat the following charm three times:

With this spell
I remain happy and well.
My loved ones dear
Will share my good cheer.

◆ Allow the tea-light to burn down and repeat the spell daily.

A blessing for a departed spirit

I wrote this spell a couple of years ago when my grandmother passed on. It helped me to come to terms with the loss and is very simple to perform.

Purpose of spell: to come to terms with a bereavement and bless the spirit that has passed over
What you need: a red or white candle and a suitable candle-holder
Moon phase: any – perform daily until after the funeral and then as often as required

◆ Light the candle (red for love or white for spirit). Focusing on the loved one who has passed over, say the following charm out loud:
Spirit fly, spirit soar;
Sorrow and pain you'll know no more.
Spirit soar, spirit fly;
Farewell only, never goodbye.
As above so below;
Your love for us will burn and glow
And light the way for all to see.
Go with our love. Blessed be!
Hear these words, hear my cry,
Spirits on the other side.
Hail and welcome now another
Who comes to rest in the arms of the Mother.

◆ Allow the candle to burn down naturally and repeat the spell as often as you need to. Remember that to witches death is not the end. It is simply a journey that takes the spirit on to a new phase of existence to await a whole new destiny.

Afterword

J hope that you have enjoyed your first steps into the Craft. You now have all the techniques, both magical and mundane, to enable you to live the life of an empowered wise woman.

In reading this book you have entered a new phase of your life. You have embarked on an amazing journey, on which you will use your inner magic and goddess power to take control of your life and shape your own destiny. Have the confidence to express yourself, to say and do what you want to do. Be proud of who you are and believe in your own talents and abilities.

Witchcraft will teach you to be all that you can be and will leave you feeling truly blessed. You are an Earth child, a daughter of the Great Goddess. Her magic flows through your veins; her power tingles in your fingertips. Use this power to improve your life and free your spirit. And know that you are taking part in a key phase in modern history – the reawakening of the Goddess!

Magic is all around you; you only have to tap into it. I trust that your life will become all that you want it to be and all that you can make it. You are now a witch. May you strive to be worthy of the title, finding joy and empowerment in your Craft.

Farewell, Earth child. May your gods go with you until our next merry meeting.

With love and bright blessings to you all!

Morgana

Further Reading

By Marie Bruce

Published by W. Foulsham & Co. Ltd

Candleburning Rituals (0-572-02692-7)
Everyday Spells for a Teenage Witch (0-572-02770-2)
How to Create a Magical Home (0-572-02963-2)
Magical Beasts (0-572-02928-4)
The Witch's Almanac 2005 (0-572-03006-1)

By Cassandra Eason

Published by W. Foulsham & Co. Ltd

Cassandra Eason's Complete Book of Spells (0-572-03001-0)
Crystal Healing (0-572-02735-4)
Crystals Talk to the Woman Within (0-572-02613-7)
Every Woman a Witch (0-572-02223-9)
Fragrant Magic (0-572-02939-X)
Magic Spells for a Happy Life (0-572-02827-X)
A Practical Guide to Witchcraft and Magick Spells (0-572-02704-4)
Runes Talk to the Woman Within (0-572-02612-9)
Smudging and Incense-burning (0-572-02737-0)
Tarot Talks to the Woman Within (0-572-025614-5)

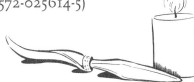

By Graham Harvey
Published by Hurst & Co. Ltd
Listening People, Speaking Earth (1-85065-272-4)

By James Lynn Page
Published by W. Foulsham & Co. Ltd
Celtic Magic (0-572-02736-2)
Native American Magic (0-572-02740-0)

By Cassie Premo Steele
Published by Ash Tree Publishing, 1999
Moon Days: creative writings about menstruation

Foulsham books are available from all good bookshops or online at
www.foulsham.com

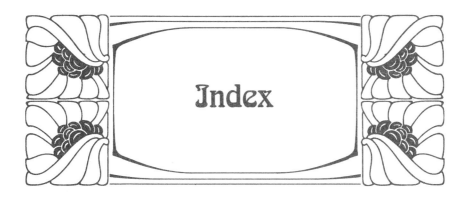

Index